HANDLEY PAGE
VICTOR

POSTWAR MILITARY AIRCRAFT: 6

HANDLEY PAGE
VICTOR

ANDREW BROOKES

LONDON

IAN ALLAN LTD

First published 1988
Reprinted 2000

ISBN 0 7110 1803 0

© Andrew Brookes 1988

Published by Ian Allan Publishing

an imprint of Ian Allan Publishing Ltd, Terminal House, Station Approach,
Shepperton, Surrey TW17 8AS.

Printed by Ian Allan Printing Ltd, Riverdene Business Park, Hersham, Surrey
KT12 4RG.

Code: 0001/A

For my daughter, Katherine

Glossary:

A&AEE	Aeroplane & Armament Experimental Establishment
AwC	Awaiting collection
C(A)	Controller (Aircraft)
conv	Conversion to
ECM	Electronic countermeasures
FF	Fire fighting
HP	Handley Page
HS	Hawker Siddeley
MoA	Ministry of Aviation
MoD(PE)	Ministry of Defence (Procurement Executive)
Min Tech	Ministry of Technology
NBS	Navigation & Bombing System
OCU	Operational Conversion Unit
P&EE	Proof & Experimental Establishment
PR	Photo-reconnaissance
RRF	Radar Reconnaissance Flight
SOC	Struck off charge
Sqn	Squadron
TTF	Tanker Training Flight
Wg	Wing

Contents

Half title:
**Victor K2 on the ramp at RAF Marham, 26 January
1988.** *Francois Prins*

Title page:
**Victor K2 XL189 displayed on the gate at RAF
Waddington on 25 March 1988.** *Francois Prins*

This page:
**Two Victor tankers from RAF Marham taking part in
an air-to-air refuelling exercise over the North Sea.**
MoD

1

The Balance on our Side

If you had delved into the *Concise Oxford Dictionary of Current English* after the Kaiser's War, you would have found the following entry:

'HANDLEY PAGE, n. Type of large aeroplane (maker).'

Not many names achieve such recognition before their owners reach middle age, and the man in question was born in Cheltenham, Gloucestershire, on 15 November 1885. Frederick Handley Page was the second of four sons of Frederick Joseph Page, proprietor of a small furniture business, and his wife Ann Eliza, née Handley. Theirs was a Plymouth Brethren household where diligence was encouraged and frivolity eschewed. By the time young Frederick entered Cheltenham Grammar School, he had acquired an extensive and apposite knowledge of the Scriptures which he was to use to telling effect in later years.

Frederick left grammar school in 1902 with a good all-round education — he remained profi-cient in Latin and Greek throughout his life — and while at Finsbury Technical College he became enamoured of the wonders of mechanical flight. Graduating in 1906, he worked first as chief designer for a firm of electrical machinery manufacturers only to leave two years later to set up business on his own account. On 17 June 1909, Handley Page became a limited liability company, which was a pretty grandiose description of a corrugated iron shed near Barking Creek. Nevertheless, the flying rights over 2½ miles of adjacent marshland were just the thing for the first British works to be constructed entirely for the manufacture of aeroplanes.

The firm started out building gliders and progressed in 1910 to a powered monoplane whose

Below:
Handley Page's first experience with a 'crescent wing' — the 'Yellow Peril' as drawn by George Volkert in 1912. The aeroplane was later designated the HP5.

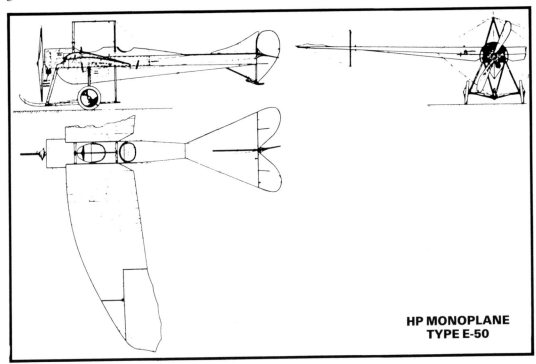

**HP MONOPLANE
TYPE E-50**

wing shape and colour caused it to be known as the Bluebird. This Type A was exhibited at the Olympia Aero Exhibition with a price tag of £375, and another monoplane — the Type D — was on show at Olympia the following year. Unfortunately it was more handsome than efficient, and Handley Page's first big success only came with the Type E, a tandem two-seat monoplane built in the hope that it might prove suitable for Army use. The Type E had swept-back wings of 35ft span and a 50hp Gnome engine which enabled it to reach 60mph. Its striking colour scheme, resulting from a liberal coating of anti-corrosive lanolin paint, caused it to be dubbed the 'Yellow Peril'.

In 1912 the company moved to larger premises at Cricklewood in North London to be close to Hendon aerodrome. Added staff were taken on and among them was George Rudolf Volkert, an Anglo-Swiss who, on graduating from North-ampton Institute, accepted Frederick's invitation to be Chief Designer at the princely salary of 15 shillings a week. The new premises at Cricklewood were designed to cope with the expansion expected following an invitation to build BE2a biplanes on behalf of the War Office.

Below:
The sharp end in World War 1 — a 1,650lb bomb underneath a Handley Page O/400. The bomber's wings are folded back because the original Admiralty specification called for an aircraft that could be housed in a shed no larger than 70ft square.

Unfortunately, only five were ordered in the first batch and the special alloy steels specified proved so difficult to obtain that delivery of the first three BE2s was severely delayed. The War Office was not impressed and when World War 1 broke out in August 1914, the Army declined Handley Page's offer of his factory and resources.

However, as the company had designed the Type L 200hp-engined biplane for Princess Ludwig of Löwenstein-Wertheim's attempt on the first direct crossing of the Atlantic, Handley Page and Volkert found themselves invited to a meeting with Cdre Murray Sueter, Director of the Admiralty Air Department. Sueter and his staff were convinced of the need for a really long-range heavy patrol bomber capable of attacking the German High Seas Fleet in Kiel before it ever put to sea. 'What we want here,' reported Cdr Charles Samson as his scratch naval squadron failed to prevent the German occupation of Antwerp, 'is a bloody paralyser to stop them in their tracks'. It was this 'bloody paralyser' that Handley Page and Volkert set out to design, and for which Sueter was to be called 'the biggest damned fool in the Navy'.

Events were to silence the critics for, by February 1915, the design of a 100ft span twin-engined biplane known as the HP11 Type 0/100 was established. The Admiralty ordered four prototypes for which Frederick insisted on an advance of £20,000. By the end of November, after the Navy had ordered another 28, the company's

7

workforce had risen to 150 and Hendon made ready for the arrival of 'the world's biggest aeroplane' which first flew on 18 December 1915.

Forty 0/100s were built and supplied to Royal Naval Air Service squadrons at Dunkirk; each aircraft carried more than a ton of bombs to attack targets inside Germany and U-boat haunts along the Belgian coast. An improved 0/400 then followed with increased fuel and bomb-carrying capacity, and in the service of the Independent Air Force they became the nocturnal bane of Rhineland towns and U-boat lairs. An 0/400 was the first aircraft to fly from Britain outside Europe — to Palestine — where Lawrence of Arabia captured the feelings of those who saw it:

'At Um el Surab, the Handley stood majestic on the grass, with Bristols and DH9As like fledgelings beneath the spread of its wings. Round it admired the Arabs saying, 'Indeed, and at last, they have sent us THE aeroplane, of which these things were foals.' Before night, rumours of Feisal's resources went over Jabel Druse and the hollow of Hauran, telling people that the balance was weighed on our side.'

But Handley Page's supreme product of the Great War was the 'Super Handley', or V/1500, designed to meet a requirement for a long-range night bomber capable of attacking distant German strategic targets including Berlin from bases in East Anglia. Working 11hr a day except Sunday afternoons, the company built the first V/1500 in six months and a trio was bombed-up at Bircham Newton ready to attack the German capital when the armistice was signed. Only a whisker prevented the 13½-ton V/1500, with its 126ft wing span and 7,500lb bomb load, from fulfilling its destiny as the world's first strategic bomber. Nevertheless the great beast vividly illustrated the remarkable progress made in four years of war, both in aeronautics and the fortunes of Handley Page. Despite his receding hairline, Frederick was still only 33 years old when he found his name in the dictionary as a synonym for large aircraft.

After 1918 Handley Page turned his attention to converting bombers into the first big airliners while at the same time realising his dream of taking the danger out of stalled flight by patenting the slotted wing. 'H.P. knows more about wings than God,' declared a rival designer, 'otherwise God would have given birds a different feather arrangement'. Be that as it may, automatic leading edge slots were adopted for all RAF aircraft in 1928, earning the company £750,000 in royalties before the patent expired.

In 1930, Handley Page's aerodrome and assembly shops were moved to Radlett in

Hertfordshire when Cricklewood airfield was sold off as a housing estate. The Heyford first saw the light of day at Radlett, followed by the Hampden which was in front line service when World War 2 began. In 1936 Handley Page received the Air Staff specification for a harder-hitting replacement for the Hampden, and Volkert's response was the HP56 twin Vulture-engined monoplane. But when the Vulture ran into development trouble, the bomber was redesigned around four Merlin engines to become the HP57 Halifax. By the same device Avro converted its inadequate Manchester into the excellent Lancaster, and for the first time Handley Page had a serious rival for the title of big bomber king.

At the Cricklewood main works 90 draughtsmen produced 13,000 aircraft drawings in time for the Halifax final design conference on Boxing Day, 1941. Altogether 6,176 Halifaxes were built in 27 versions by 51,000 men and women in 41 group factories and 600 sub-contractors' works between 1941 and 1946. At the peak of production in 1944, between 38-42 Halifaxes were turned out every month by the 500 or so final assembly and flight test employees at Radlett. In addition to coastal, heavy transport, paratroop and glider-towing duties, the Halifax provided over 40% of Britain's total heavy bomber power during World War 2 with the 68,000lb Mk VI being capable of 2,350 miles range and a bomb load of 6½ tons. It is undeniable that the Halifax was overshadowed by the Lancaster in the popular mind, but the crews of the 76 'Halibag' squadrons eventually established in Bomber Command had much to be grateful for in its robust construction and viceless ease of operation. In producing one of World War 2's winners, Frederick Handley Page richly deserved the knighthood bestowed upon him by a grateful nation in 1942.

Left:
A HP15 V/1500 in all its glory at Cricklewood in June 1918. The V/1500's wing area of 2,800sq ft was 200ft larger than that of the biggest Victor.

2
Victor Nascent

At the end of World War 2, Sir Frederick was still very much in charge of his firm but the days had gone whereby any individual could summon up a military aeroplane on his own. As late as 1937, 'H.P.' would come down to the mock-ups on his shopfloor and declare imperiously and authoritatively that bits should be removed here or added there, but the war expanded aeronautics far beyond a one-man show. Yet Sir Frederick was still very astute and remained involved in all aspects of his company. His influence was large, and because he was on nodding terms with men such as Churchill, 'H.P.' represented his firm in the corridors of power and acted as salesman for the Hastings military and Hermes civil transport versions of the Halifax while his subordinates concentrated on turning metal into flying machines.

George Volkert was Chief Designer through both world wars but advanced design went hand in hand with advanced research. In 1929, 'H.P.' brought Gustav Victor Lachmann, a former German air force pilot and later chief designer with Schneider and Albatross, into the company where he was eventually given charge of a separate design team at Edgware. When war came, it was discovered that the absent-minded Lachmann had neglected to get himself naturalised, and because officialdom could not allow a German national to work on the latest means of bombing his homeland, the good doctor found himself interned for the duration on the Isle of Man.

Yet 'Gus' Lachmann's talents were not wasted during his sojourn. After 1943 he was allowed to communicate with his deputy in the Research Department, Godfrey Lee, to help resume work on a private venture swept-wing tailless research aircraft designed before the war to overcome the problems of drag and centre of gravity displacement caused by heavy tail armament. Aircraft, especially bombers, get attacked mainly from the rear but conventional bombers such as the Halifax could not carry large rear turrets because that would make them tail-heavy. Neither could the turret operate effectively from the mid-position because the tail and fin got in the way, but if the tail was removed, the aircraft would

not need such a large fuselage and the turret could be positioned near the centre of gravity with an uninterrupted arc of fire. It was all good stuff and before he was interned, Lachmann's fertile brain had conceived the two-seat twin-pusher HP75 which first flew in August 1943. The little aircraft had swept wings with a fin and rudder on each tip, and it was christened 'Manx' because Manx cats have no tails (and perhaps as an oblique reference to Lachmann in his distant abode). The Manx flew for about 18hr before terrible vibration caused parts to fall off, but although it was a World War 2 concept with no reference to high Mach number research, the Manx did point Handley Page in the direction of tailless sweep and the company had ideas for a tailless bomber weighing 70 tons by the beginning of 1943. When the war ended, Volkert, who had not been well for some time, retired. He was replaced as Chief Designer by his Assistant, Reginald Stafford, while Lachmann returned from exile to take charge of special projects in research, design and development.

The Avro Lincoln replaced the Lancaster and Halifax as the RAF's primary big bomber in 1945. This was a time of great change because the development of the atomic bomb had revolutionised military thinking, and the Attlee Government's decision in January 1947 to develop a British atomic bomb was inevitable. The most effective and economical means of delivering such a weapon was by a bomber powered by jet engines, which meant flying at heights and speeds greatly in excess of those of the Lincoln. When English Electric tendered successfully for their Canberra twin Avon-engined jet bomber to replace the Mosquito, Sir Frederick was so confident that a similar replacement would be needed for the Lincoln in five or six years' time that he issued a confidential memorandum on 14 June 1945 requesting an immediate investigation into two classes of bomber: one was of 100,000lb all-up weight with four Avon-sized turbojets (or two of twice that size), and the other was a 60,000lb twin Avon creation, but both were

Right:
The HP75 Manx as designed by Dr Gustav Lachmann.

to make use of the experience gained with the tailless Manx.

The bulk of the initial research work fell on the firm's Research Engineer, Godfrey Lee, who had joined Handley Page from Saunders-Roe in 1937. He was responsible for future projects and as the Germans had led the field in high speed aeronautical research up to then, Lee was sent as the company's representative on a mission to study German tailless aircraft projects in October 1945. The 32-year-old Lee spent his time talking mostly to research engineers and aerodynamicists at the Völkenrode experimental establishment near Brunswick and at the old university town of Göttingen. 'It was there we found out the true story of what wing sweep could do for you, namely that you could have a sensible thickness/chord ratio of 10-12% and still fly at Mach 0.8 upwards without serious drag rise.'

On his return home, Lee contracted pneumonia and had to go into hospital. It was during his enforced convalescence that he put all his new-found knowledge into a feasibility study for a 50-seat, 50-ton high-subsonic transatlantic airliner known as the HP72. Looking back, Lee regards it as a 'dreadful thing' with a great big body and swept wings, but the HP72 reflected the uncertainty of the times. High speed jets demanded totally different strengths and tolerances from those employed previously; it was like the transition from biplane to monoplane all over again with a revolutionary new engine technology to complicate the issue. The scale of the task is best summed up by the fact that the only component common to both the Halifax and the Victor was a rubber bung.

Although the company abandoned the HP72 in January 1946, the designations HP72A and HP75A were used to cover Lee's investigations into a possible high speed bomber (with an alternative transport role) of 90,000lb all-up weight powered by four Avon engines. The

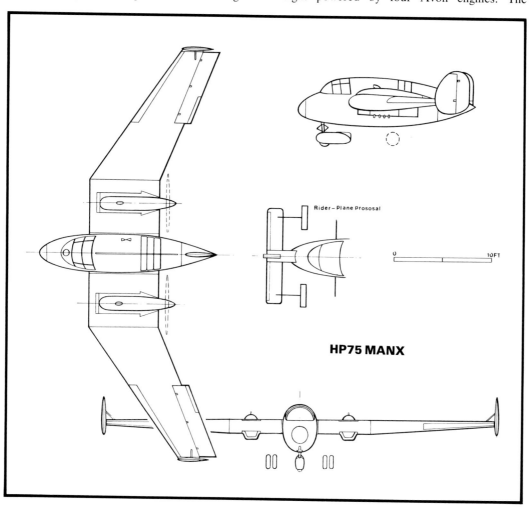

Rider—Plane Prososal

HP75 MANX

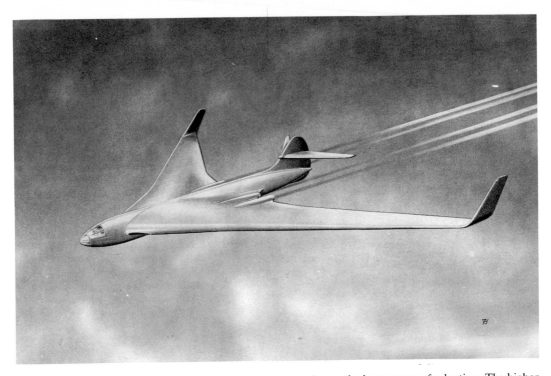

HP75A, with front rider-plane control, was quickly ruled out in favour of the HP72A which had 45° swept wings and tip rudders plus a small swept tailplane with elevators to balance nose-down pitching moments caused by flap lowering at low speed or compressibility at high speed. Knowing nothing as yet of Air Ministry thinking on the subject, Lee put forward a proposal on 25 February 1946 for an aircraft powered by four Avons with a 122ft span, a wing area of 2,100sq ft, an aspect ratio of seven and a wing loading of 43lb/sq ft to carry a 10,000lb bomb at 520kt over a still air range of 5,000 miles. Two days later Stafford approved the proposal and a brochure was prepared to demonstrate the aircraft's potential as a bomber with alternative applications as a cargo or passenger transport. The aircraft was rechristened HP80 and the brochure sent to the RAF's Director of Operational Requirements, Gp Capt Silyn-Roberts.

The HP80 was so much in keeping with current RAF studies that Silyn-Roberts and his deputy, Gp Capt Cooper, visited Cricklewood on 19 July to discuss the Air Staff's requirements for a long-range bomber. In their view, height and speed were the best means of salvation. The higher a bomber flew, the harder it would be to catch, and the faster it travelled, the less time it would be exposed to detection and attack. It must be remembered that in those days very little was known about operations around the speed of sound. Not a few experts believed that Mach 1 was a barrier that man crossed at his peril, so if the RAF went for an attacker that could fly in the stratosphere at the brink of the sonic barrier, it would force an opponent to cross and re-cross this hazard as he tried to intercept. Thus the idea of a sleek HP80 stripped of turrets and armour appealed to the RAF. The only changes proposed by Silyn-Roberts and Cooper were insurances such as a visual bombing station in case radar bombsights could not be produced in time, an engineer's station pending simplification of the engine controls, facilities for an electronic counter-measures operator in a separate pressure cabin near the tail and, if possible, a jettisonable main pressure cabin.

On 2 November, a number of Ministry research staff visited Cricklewood to discuss radar equipment for the new bomber. Later marks of Halifax had carried the self-contained radar device codenamed 'H2S' which made use of the fact that water, open country and built-up areas (including individual large buildings) produce distinctly different radar echoes. Unrolling radar maps of terrain beneath a Halifax could be created before the crews' very eyes which enabled them to navigate and bomb with precision under cover of darkness. The main weapon-aiming and primary fixing aid of the V-bombers was to be the Navigation & Bombing System (NBS). Its centrepiece was to be the H2S Mk 9 radar, designed to meet a specification that demanded twice the accuracy at twice the height and speed of its wartime predecessors. The Mk 9 scanner was to be 6ft long and it was to rotate horizontally inside a large radome below the HP80's flightdeck floor: altogether, the Ministry wanted Handley Page to accommodate 1,500lb of radar equipment with all aerials to be suppressed.

All these details were pulled together into the final draft of Air Staff Operational Requirement (OR) 229 which was circulated on 7 November 1946. Once OR 229 was approved, it was translated into Specification B35/46 which, when issued on 24 January 1947, called for a 'day and night medium range bomber landplane capable of carrying a 10,000lb bomb to a target 1,500 nautical miles from a base which may be anywhere in the world'. Cruising speed was to be 500kt/575mph (equated to Mach 0.873 in the stratosphere) at maximum continuous cruising power, and the aircraft was to be capable of reaching 45,000ft after 1hr and 50,000ft within 2½hr of take-off. Ability to climb above 50,000ft was desirable but not essential.

As the aircraft was expected to bomb at its operational ceiling in all weather conditions, Spec B35/46 foresaw that 'the majority of bombing will be done with the target hidden by cloud and darkness. It is therefore necessary to carry the new radar bombing equipment, now under development, which makes use of all radar and Dead Reckoning navigational data to feed the bombing computer. When the target can be seen, however, a visual bombsight, fed from the same bombing computer, will be used and the provision of a good visual bomb-aiming position is of great importance. . . . It must be possible to release bombs at any speed at which the aircraft is capable of flying'. The aircraft was 'to rely on speed, height and evasive manoeuvre for protection against interception. It will not carry orthodox defensive armament, but will be equipped with early warning devices to enable effective avoiding manoeuvres to be made and radar countermeasures to deflect a beam on which a controlled weapon may be launched against it'.

The crew of five — two pilots, two navigators/bomb aimers and a signaller — were to be housed in a single pressure cabin. The cabin was to be large enough to allow each member of the crew to move from his seat during flight. The cabin pressure was not to be below the equivalent of 8,000ft on the flight to and from the target, but provision was required for it to be reduced to the equivalent of 25,000ft in the combat zone. The complete pressure cabin had to be jettisonable if abandonment proved necessary.

Spec B35/46 preferred that the aircraft had not less than four and not more than six engines and stipulated that it must be operable from existing bomber airfields. 'The maximum weight when fully loaded ought, therefore, not to exceed 100,000lb', though this limitation was raised to 115,000lb after pleas from the aircraft industry. 'Catapult or trolley launching is not acceptable, nor is arrester gear for landing.' The whole aircraft was to be suitable for the economic production of at least 500 airframes at a maximum rate of not less than 10 per month.

The Specification arrived when Handley Page was primarily concerned with the bread-and-butter work of producing Hastings and Hermes, so Reggie Stafford left the HP80 to germinate in the New Projects Group. This Group was led by Charles Joy, an ex-Armstrong Whitworth and Gloster draughtsman who was appointed Assistant Chief Designer in 1947 at the age of 36. His Group thrashed out the aerodynamics of the HP80 early in 1947 though Sir Fred and Doc Lachmann were very much in on the discussions. 'Sir Frederick couldn't have sat down and calculated the pressure distribution on the wing', recalled Godfrey Lee, 'and you wouldn't have expected him to. But he knew how it was being done and what it was all about.'

The essence of Lee's problem was wing drag: the lower the drag, the higher the aircraft's economic cruise speed and the greater its range. As the main drag would come from the wing, he needed to produce a wing with low drag at high speed but also one which was controllable and stable at the stall so that a normal pilot could land safely at a reasonable speed.

Godfrey Lee began by deciding that B35/46 needed a wing of fairly high sweep and relatively high aspect ratio. Handley Page's great rival in the advanced bomber competition chose a different path with their delta-winged Avro 698, where the low aspect ratio was partially offset by a big wing area which kept the span up to a reasonable value. Stafford recalled that they considered using a delta shape but his team did not like the stability problems they anticipated (wrongly as it happened) would go with it. However, high sweep combined with high aspect ratio produced a number of problems for Handley Page. For a start swept wings tend to stall first at their tips, and, because these are well aft of the centre of gravity, the overall centre of pressure moves further forward and the resulting unstable state of affairs would cause the aircraft to pitch up dangerously. High aspect ratio also imposes considerable structural strain because the lift produced at the wingtip can be transferred to the fuselage via the wing root attachments which may be 50ft ahead of the tip, thereby setting up a strong twisting moment.

The New Projects Group could not solve these problems by going for a low aspect ratio wing because this would only increase the induced drag; in addition, a long-range bomber needed a high lift/drag ratio to operate at the altitudes that only a wing of high aspect ratio with considerable span, and hence wing area, could provide. However, they could have the best of both worlds if the wing was tapered from an inboard section of maximum sweepback, to minimise frontal drag and compressibility, out to a tip of no more than moderate sweep to preclude the chances of tip stall. With the load on the wingtip now brought forward of the wing axis, the tendency to twist would also be prevented by a strong opposite torsion from the inner wing so that the wing incidence remained unchanged no matter how much it was bent upwards by flight loads. The bonus for Handley Page here was that their flying controls were not now behind the flexural axis as on other swept-wing aircraft, but were slightly ahead so they did not suffer from reversal caused by wing twisting.

The wing inboard section was therefore swept back at a very sharp angle of 53° on quarter chord, with a root thickness/chord ratio of 16% for structural strength and to provide adequate stowage room for engines and undercarriage. The wingtip on the other hand had 22° sweep and a thickness/chord ratio of 8%, but this was acceptable because there were no stowage problems here and it was the least lightly loaded part of the structure. In between it was decided that it was too dramatic to go from 53° to 22° in one giant step, so Lee put in an intermediate section of around 35° to blend the two extremities together. The result was a 100ft-span wing of around 2,000sq ft area on which each semi-span had three angles of sweep, with changes of sweep or 'kinks' equally spaced. 'Perhaps it is simpler to say', recorded Lee, 'that from a tip stall point of view, the wing is equivalent to one with 30-35° sweep, but that by having more sweep at the root we cashed in on the big advantage of greater thickness where it mattered at the small price of a thinner than otherwise outer wing. We actually did it that rather long-winded way as you sometimes tend to do when you start on things.'

This then was the crescent wing, combining all the features of a swept-back thick wing and an unswept wing in one aerofoil, with the added advantage that by varying the wing thickness along with sweep, it was possible to maintain a constant critical Mach number from root to tip. Critical Mach number is the airspeed at which shock waves

first form and what Lee wanted was an aircraft shape wherein all the components, be they nose, wings or fin, would accelerate the air flow by the same amount everywhere such that they would all form shock waves simultaneously with no part being especially affected. Handley Page's small team of aerodynamicists — men such as Jack Housego, Stanley Newport, Bob Annenberg and Frank Davies — designed every square inch of the external shape of the HP80 to ensure a uniform pressure distribution. 'We couldn't take the design out of a book', observed Lee, 'so we used the best methods available based on work done by the National Physical Laboratory — methods no one would use nowadays but we had no computers then, only little hand-turned machines. We did all the calculations by simple methods but we did them.'

The compound sweep or crescent wing concept was not entirely new — Dipl Ing R. E. Kosin, Arado's chief aerodynamicist, had come up with the same answer when called upon to produce a high speed wing for the Arado 234 jet bomber. The Arado 234 V16 embodied an inboard leading edge angled at 35°, decreasing in two stages to 25°, and it is popularly believed that Lee discovered this wing on his visit to Germany in 1945. This is not so. Lee never visited any aircraft firm apart from that of the Horten Brothers at Göttingen who built the Gotha 229, the world's first pure flying wing jet bomber, and he certainly never heard of the Arado design. 'The one real concept we got out of the German visit was that sweep was a good thing', Lee later recalled, 'and the crescent wing on the HP80 was evolved by ourselves at Handley Page. It did not arise from anything Arado or anybody else did.'

It is open to debate whether the HP80 planform should more accurately be termed a scimitar or a cusp rather than a crescent, but this wing was undoubtedly the most efficient high-subsonic wing on any drawing board in 1947. Lee obviously made the shape work but 'I couldn't tell you who first suggested it, even though I was so intimately concerned with it'. Charles Joy also denied any credit for the idea, which just seemed to him to

Right:
The Victor's 'kissing cousin', the podded-engined B-47. The Victor had almost the same weight, span and parasitic drag but it had the advantage of 50% more wing area to reach greater height. Even if altitude had not been a prime consideration, Handley Page could not have opted for a small-section, thick-skinned B-47 type wing while remaining within the original 100,000lb weight limitation. Nevertheless, in the final all-up weight stakes, both B-47 and Victor were to be classed as 'medium' bombers and the V-force known as the Medium Bomber Force; the huge B-52 on the other hand was a 'heavy' bomber.

emerge out of discussions between the New Projects Group, Lachmann and Sir Frederick. But anyone who compares the planform of the 'Yellow Peril', built before Godfrey Lee was born, with that of the HP80, cannot fail to see the family likeness. 'It would never surprise me', said Joy, 'if Frederick Handley Page wasn't himself responsible for the crescent wing concept.'

By spring 1947 the HP80 had evolved around the crescent wing with upturned tips culminating in vertical fins, plus a swept tailplane on an almost non-existent stub fin at the rear of a slender circular-section fuselage with a maximum diameter of 9ft 10in. The all-moving tailplane, swept at 45°, was small at 150sq ft but it was only intended for automatic trimming purposes when the flaps were lowered. Lateral and longitudinal manoeuvres were to be controlled by large elevons occupying the outer halves of the wing trailing edge, with leading edge slots in front of them (what else from Handley Page?) to give good low speed stalling characteristics.

The New Projects Group calculated that in view of the very large wind tunnel test programme involved, the prototype could not be expected to fly before 1951. Joy proposed to begin the drawing office programme on 1 October 1947, allowing 21 months to June 1949 for the basic layout and 30 months to March 1950 for completion of the powered flying control system. All drawings for the first prototype as a flying shell could be completed by June 1951, and additional drawings for the fully-equipped version would be issued by March 1952. First flight dates were scheduled for March 1952 as a flying shell and September 1952 fully equipped. It was a tight programme for such a relatively small design organisation, but 'impossible' was a word rarely uttered in Sir Frederick's hearing and the HP80 design scheme was submitted to the Ministry in May 1947 in competition with five other firms.

The HP80, as tendered, was designed around four Metrovick F9 engines nominally rated at 7,500lb thrust. The F9 was the largest turbojet then running in the world and in Lee's opinion, it was 'unquestionably the best engine available at the time'. He and Joy were equally convinced that the engines should be buried in the wing roots. Across the Atlantic, Boeing was to give its B-47 and B-52 podded engines but there was never any intention that Handley Page would do likewise. 'We had to meet a high cruising altitude of 50,000ft', said Lee, 'whereas the B-47 only had to operate at 40,000ft, if it could get there.' His short answer to anyone who asks why Handley Page did not go for podded engines in 1947 is that the B-47 and HP80 were very similar in weight and span but that the HP80 had 50% more wing area for the same amount of induced and parasitic drag. 'In fact, we couldn't have got to 50,000ft with less wing area and having got that wing area and crescent shape, we had enough depth at the wing

15

root to put the engines in. It would have been silly to do anything else in the circumstances.'

No one would dream of fitting engine intakes into 53° of sweep today. Nearly 1,000lb of thrust would be found to be blanked off the outboard engines of the production HP80 when standing still at take-off power because the air flow concentrated at the outer corner of the intake: the aircraft had to roll well down the runway before the missing thrust was gathered back. But Handley Page did not realise this in 1947 and it went ahead because of very encouraging results obtained at Göttingen with such an arrangement. 'Perhaps we were the only firm brave enough or daft enough to do it', said Lee, but pods meant induced drag, not to mention larger fins and rudders to cope with asymmetric flight, when the aim was to achieve the cleanest profile possible. If the designers could not get rid of drag caused by the airflow meeting the large wing root, it made sense to let some of it pass through the engines that fitted snugly into the 6ft-deep HP80 wing root.

Meanwhile an Advanced Bomber Project Group at Farnborough was trying to evaluate the six designs tendered for Spec B35/46. When the too futuristic and the too staid were rejected, the Group was left to choose between the HP80 and the Avro 698. It was not easy. High speed wind tunnel tests showed, for example, that the drag coefficient of the crescent wing was about double that of the delta but as the wing area of the former was only half that of the Avro 698, the figures were comparable for a given weight. The Group then found that the Air Staff restriction on maximum weight to 100,000lb, and then 115,000lb, was self-defeating in that if wing area could be increased, and wing loading thereby reduced, a bomber could fly higher. Thus if the weight of the HP80 was allowed to grow to 150,000lb, the potential height over target could be raised from about 50,000ft to 53,500ft. The Group felt that such a benefit was worth the extra tons of concrete necessary to make longer and stronger runways, and the RAF agreed.

Nevertheless, after considering all the evidence, the Group had to conclude that 'because of the present uncertainty in basic information, we cannot put all our eggs into one basket. Several designs must be chosen to spread the risk'. Thus the Group opted for both projects, the HP80 because it was considered to be potentially best in terms of height over target (53,500ft) but also the Avro 698 because even though it only promised to reach 48,500ft, it would be much more manoeuvrable when it got there. The two designs complemented each other but the aerodynamics of both were still so uncertain that the Project Group had to recommend both in case one turned out to possess some ghastly fault that would render it

unworkable. In fact the RAF was also to order the Vickers Valiant in April 1948 as a simpler 'insurance' aircraft in case both advanced bombers failed to live up to expectations.

Once all this was decided, Handley Page received its Instruction to Proceed on 1 January 1948. This was a sort of holding action which demonstrated that the Ministry was willing to pay £50,000 for further development work but not ready to go as far as issuing production contracts. It was at this stage that the rest of the firm's specialists, who had previously been drawn into the New Projects Group's discussions only in a consultative capacity, were officially brought into the project. Charles Joy was put in charge of the HP80, although the whole design team had progress meetings with Sir Fred and Reggie Stafford every fortnight, while Godfrey Lee, who was by now chief aerodynamicist, saw his team expanded from a miniscule half-dozen to a comparatively extravagant total of 20 or more souls.

One thing they did dispose of quickly was the wingtip fins. Sir Fred had never really liked them, believing that shock waves might form on one and not the other causing the aircraft to yaw. Although Lee did not agree he was glad to see the back of them because he had more than enough unorthodox features to keep him busy. The wingtip fins were officially deleted from the HP80 on 14 January 1948, allowing Lee to increase the wing span from 100ft to 110ft. As research had shown that more fin area was needed, the design team added an orthodox fin and rudder with a tailplane on the advice of Farnborough who felt it was essential to minimise the effect of aeroelastic distortion.

The new fin and rudder added a weight penalty of 500lb but this was partially offset in March when a four-wheeled bogie main undercarriage, retracting rearwards outboard of the outer engine bays, was substituted for the large inward-retracting single main wheels proposed at the tender stage. The bogies were some 300lb lighter. Three months later, the decision was taken to lift the tail to the top of the fin on the recommendation of Doc Lachmann, partly based on experience with the Hastings which suffered from the destabilising effect of slipstream at low speeds, but mainly to lift it out of the turbulent jet wake. The original all-moving tailplane was abandoned for structural reasons, to be replaced by a very small fixed tailplane — 'really just something to hold the hinge brackets', said Lee — and a very large elevator. In fact 90% of the two-stage sweep tailplane was elevator, the theory being that as the HP80 was going to be wholly power-controlled, it might as well have the next best thing to an all-moving tailplane which would cut down that insidious enemy, drag. Even so, the tailplane had doubled in size thereby eliminating the need for the ailerons to act together as elevons when the flaps were lowered, and its span was only 11in shorter than that of the Hawker Hunter mainplane it resembled.

The overall design concept of the HP80 having been agreed with the Ministry, Cricklewood now turned its attention to scaled-down flying models. A design study for a radio-controlled one-third scale glider, the HP87, was abandoned when it was flown into the ground during its first outing, but on 12 March 1948 Spec E6/48 was issued for a flying test model having HP80 wings and tail scaled down to 0.4 full size. Designated HP88, the mini-crescent was intended to be built around a Supermarine Swift fuselage because its fuel tanks were compatible with 45° sweep at the wing root. 'It was all part of the state of thinking at the time', said Ken Pratt, who was to run the Test House and experimental workshop from which HP80 flying took place. 'It was such a big step and such a large aircraft that the firm needed some information to be going on with from the model. It was the same with Avro — we all felt that we had to break down the big step from drawing board to prototype.'

The aim of the HP88 therefore was to explore the behaviour of the crescent wing at high and low speeds, the effect of depressing the flaps, and the degree of stability imparted by the high tailplane. Unfortunately there was insufficient drawing office capacity at Cricklewood to do the detail design of the scaled-down wing and tail, so this was sub-contracted to General Aviation Ltd of Feltham, Middlesex. General Aviation's weight estimates were agreed on 26 April. Two days later the Ministry awarded a contract to build two HP80 prototypes, WB771 and WB775, with Metrovick 9 engines; the first was now expected to fly in May 1952 and the second six months later.

When Metrovick opted out of the aero-engine business in October 1948, development of the F9 turbojet was transferred to Armstrong Siddeley Motors at Coventry: the engine was then named Sapphire. First runs confirmed that it could be scaled up by 25% to give 9,000lb static thrust and the Sapphire was chosen for production as the HP80 powerplant in May 1948. By then, General Aviation Ltd had merged with Blackburn Aircraft Ltd and the mini-crescent project moved up to Brough on Humberside where approval to construct one HP88, VX330, was received in June.

At Brough the hybrid was known as the Blackburn YB2 while Supermarine got into the act by calling it the Supermarine Type 521, but whichever designation was used, the HP88 was more of a sow's ear than a silk purse. It took to the

Above and Below:

The HP88 posing for publicity photographs at Carnaby in June 1951. The Ministry of Supply chose to release this exact side view so that the 'classified' crescent wing could not be seen. An artist has even airbrushed the shadow to make it look like a plain swept wing.
BAe

air from Carnaby in glossy royal blue on 21 June 1951 at the hands of Blackburn's chief test pilot, 'Sailor' Parker, who found it very easy to fly. But the crescent wing flying that day reflected the original HP80 concept, being roughly divided into equal thirds of sweep with a 2 : 1 taper ratio, whereas by 1951 this planform had undergone considerable modification back at Cricklewood. All Handley Page men pay tribute to the 'invaluable' help they received from the National

Above:
The glossy blue VX330 in the air looking very much like the cross between a Swift and an Attacker that it was. Span and length were 40ft, gross weight was 14,460lb, and top speed was Mach 0.9. Some 2,000 changes took place in HP80 design before much metal was cut, not one of which resulted from HP88 findings.

Physical Laboratory and the Royal Aircraft Establishment (RAE) at Farnborough, and one of the things the latter discovered in its high speed wind tunnel at the beginning of 1948 was that drag started to increase rapidly at Mach 0.8 on the crescent instead of after the design cruising speed of Mach 0.875. This was caused by the outer wing being too thick, so Lee took 2% off the tip thickness/chord ratio, bringing it down to 6%, which seemed good enough until the structures men demanded a thicker wing root to accommodate their engines, fuel tanks and undercarriage. In the end the root got so big that the wing had a taper ratio of 4 : 1 and when this was put in the wind tunnel there was nothing they could do to make it have a sensible stall. The delays caused by all this were now getting quite serious so Lee took a gamble and added 20% to the outer wing chord to reduce the taper ratio once more; fortunately, this solution worked though it moved the outer kink inboard. 'Aerodynamicists always have to find a way out of the other man's problems', declared Lee philosophically.

Even so, leading edge flaps eventually had to be added to the outer half of the span because the thicker outer wing had an adverse effect on tip stalling. Wind tunnel tests showed that the stall, if it came, could be pretty vicious so after a very complicated and expensive programme, the firm developed great accumulators of stored energy which thumped these leading edge flaps down within a second on a signal from a pressure ratio switch which calculated lift coefficient from

tappings above and below the wing. With the addition of dihedral to the tailplane to effectively increase fin area and thereby improve directional stability, this became the final layout of the HP80.

The HP80 wing and flaps were therefore quite different from the real thing by the time VX330 first flew. Its tailplane was also pivoted some way down the fin, which was bad enough except that by the time Supermarine delivered its fuselage to Brough on 25 February 1950, the all-moving tailplane and elevons had been discarded from the HP80 in favour of normal elevators and ailerons. The HP88 on the other hand retained elevons and 'slab' tailplane, plus airbrakes which were uncharacteristic of the HP80 in both form and location.

In fact the mini-crescent with its unrepresentative wing, tail, controls, Nene engine and tailwheel, plus its fuselage that had now become that of an Attacker with Swift wing roots, fuel system and instrument layout, had almost become a separate design problem; in effect it was running parallel to rather than as part of the HP80 programme. 'The best we could have got out of it', admits Ken Pratt, 'was some free information on how the aircraft was going to fly. It wasn't going to

19

influence much design work.' As Avro found with their scaled-down version of the delta, the HP88 flew too late and was too unrepresentative to affect a prototype that was well on its way to construction, even if it had not crashed killing Handley Page test pilot Duggie Broomfield on 26 August 1951. By then VX330 had amassed 14 flying hours and Broomfield had been briefed to carry out stick jerk tests in preparation for the HP88's debut at the Farnborough Show that year. He approached Stansted runway after 10min flying at about 300ft in a high speed shallow dive when the aircraft was seen to pull into a steep climb before disintegrating. Broomfield ejected too late and he was found dead in his seat, the 32nd test pilot to die in the UK since 1945.

VX330's tailplane fell some distance away from the main wreckage, and all the evidence pointed to structural failure through overstress, but the accident occurred because an inertial coupling between the powered controls and the elevator had imposed a strain of 12g on the little aircraft causing it to break up. Ironically, the fault involved the bob-weight fitted as a 'g' restrictor for safety reasons on the instructions of RAE. It was some consolation that neither the controls nor the tail unit they controlled were the same as those on the HP80, so the accident did not delay the development of the bomber VX330 was meant to represent. But it must be concluded that the HP88 programme was not worth a man's life and the £1.8 million spent on it, even if there was some spin-off for Blackburn when it came to designing its Buccaneer. By August 1952 the two HP80 prototypes were so well advanced that the question of funding a second scaled-down test model was quietly put to rest.

3

Victor Emergent

It was in constructing the HP80 that Charles Joy came into his own. Structures were Joy's forte and being in day-to-day charge of the HP80 programme, he controlled the various line management functions that were necessary to build a successful bomber. 'Lee's earlier work on the shape', recalled a colleague, 'was responsible for the fact that it was not like the Valiant, Vulcan or anything else, but there is little doubt that Joy was the motivating power that turned it into a Victor in the end.'

Surface finish was one of the primary concerns of Joy and his Chief Stressman, Ray Sandifer. 'The shape was everything', said Ken Pratt; 'we went for all the things that were good for giving low drag'. Windows, bulges and other excrescences were anathema and were only tolerated if operational needs had to override aerodynamic cleanliness. Pratt remembers that they fought tooth and nail for aerodynamic excellence in the early days: 'to get the structure in place, small concessions were made; to get the systems in, practically no concessions were made'.

Construction of the HP80 was no easy matter because it was bound to be heavier than an orthodox swept-wing aircraft and therefore the closest possible attention had to be paid to detail to save weight. Fuel tankage was a case in point. One proviso of Spec B35/46 was that 'tanks must be so arranged or compartmented that one hole does not cause the loss of more than 10% of remaining fuel'. To meet the 'ten per cent rule', Handley Page had a much more difficult task in trying to cram 40 tons of fuel into the available internal space than their rivals Avro who had a vast delta wing to play with. The HP80 finished up with 29 flexible Marflex crashproof fuel tanks all of which were pressurised to prevent boiling at high altitude, but putting tanks pressurised up to 20lb/sq in into the wings caused another problem. Joy decided very early on that the solution was to opt for sandwich construction, which not only resisted pressure and did not wrinkle under load but also allowed thin skin materials to be employed at their widest distance apart for ordering and load bending and to resist torsion.

For three years Handley Page tried to construct a wing made out of honeycomb sandwiches — two stress-bearing skins separated by honeycomb material such as Dufaylite and held together by adhesives. Chance Vought and Martins were already working along similar lines in the USA when Sir Frederick and Godfrey Lee visited them in 1949, and for a time the adhesive Araldite looked so promising that it was decided to make a pair of sandwich wings for flight testing on a Miles Messenger under the designation HP93. However, when the firm came to test its honeycomb under high humidity, the adhesive appeared to lose its strength and there were fears that the structure might fall to bits. It was easy to get cold feet about adhesives when aiming for a 5,000hr airframe life, and in Lee's opinion the edge of the wing spar structure was already carrying too great a load for anyone to have any great confidence in stabilising it with bits of glued honeycomb. By then research time was running out and prototypes had to be built, so Joy went for a structure making extensive use of sandwich panels consisting of accurately contoured outer and inner aluminium-alloy sheets spot-welded to a light alloy core corrugated span-wise.

This alternative to honeycomb was devised by Ray Sandifer and it represented a radical departure given the long-standing distrust of welding by British airworthiness authorities. Spot-welding consisted of passing very heavy current through two surfaces so that they melted together to give a strong, rigid joint. The new sandwich design saved weight because the double-skinned panels needed no stringers and could be easily riveted or bolted to wing ribs and fuselage frames: it was a much better technical solution than honeycomb because there were now three skins instead of two to carry the many tons per square inch of end loads. Using photo-lofted templates — a process pioneered by Handley Page on the Halifax — sandwich panels were quickly manufactured to a high degree of interchangeability: these panels, being self-supporting to a great extent, could then be joined into sub-assemblies without the usual large array of jigs and fixtures. The process needed over 500,000 spot-welds for each HP80 to get a smooth finish, but a great deal of weight as well as human effort was saved in eliminating thousands of rivets in the

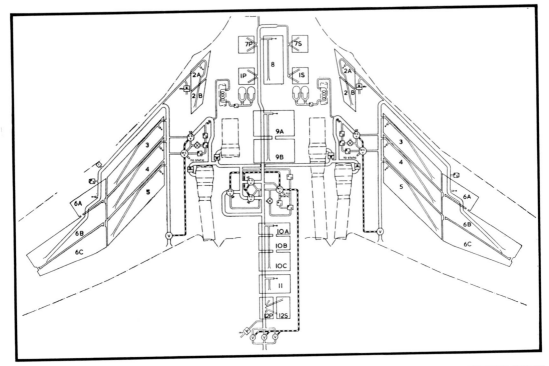

The fuel venting system on the Victor showing the layout of 29 individual internal wing and fuselage fuel tanks.

outer skin. After X-ray inspection of the spot-welds — and every spot-weld had to be X-rayed in the beginning until stringent quality control allowed production panels to be random-sampled — the inner flanges were blind-riveted to inner skins where surface finish was less important.

The finished mainplane comprised an inner wing housing the engines in its inboard portion and the undercarriage outboard, an outer wing carrying the ailerons and nose flaps, and a transport joint in between. Basically the wing was a multi-spar structure with multiple torsion boxes formed by load-carrying skins. The HP80 differed from the Vickers Valiant and Avro delta in having its strong wing box entirely ahead of the engines so that the most highly stressed part of the aircraft was removed from possible fire damage. Nor was it weakened by large access doors and the wing was capable of easier adaptation to bigger engines.

The HP80 fuselage was built in three major sub-assemblies; front, combined centre and rear, and tail cone. The front fuselage, extending back to a point roughly in line with the wing leading edge, started life in the words of one Cricklewood man as 'just a delicate shape'. It was then adapted to accommodate the H2S scanner and prone visual bombing station plus cloud and collision warning radar.

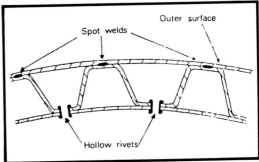

Above:
The corrugated skin of the Victor.

Next came the crew pressure cabin which was to become a subject of much discussion. The first version of the Operational Requirement had given designers the freedom to choose between one or two pilots, but Spec B35/46 finalised on two in case the captain was incapacitated in action. Although the Specification sought maximum crew comfort to reduce fatigue, it also attached particular importance to keeping the size and hence the vulnerability of the pressure cabin as small as possible. Thus no equipment that could be remotely controlled was to be carried in the cabin and the original idea of locating the Electronic Counter-measures (ECM) operator aft was never heard of again. The cabin pressure flow was also to be such that it would maintain an equivalent of 25,000ft at maximum cruising altitude, assuming a 1in diameter hole for every 12sq ft of projected area.

Despite official preference for a jettisonable crew capsule, the Handley Page tender design provided ejection seats for all five crew members. Peter Cronbach masterminded the original cockpit layout whereby the first pilot's seat on the port side was staggered slightly in front of the co-pilot's on the starboard. The two navigators had forward-facing seats behind the co-pilot while, slightly ahead of them on the port side, came the radio/ECM operator also facing forward. All seats were on the same level and lightweight armour-plate sheets were proposed to give protection from stern attack. Nevertheless, the Air Staff clung to their desire for a jettisonable capsule. In part this was to compress the cabin by making the roof available for instrumentation and controls, but it also stemmed from the fact that in 1947 no one had much idea of what it would be like to fly at 50,000ft, let alone the effects on men dangling at the end of parachutes at such rarified levels. 'The problem of the escape of the crew from a pressure cabin of an aircraft travelling at high speed presents many difficulties', declared a Farnborough study in February 1948. Use of an ejection seat at 50,000ft and 500kt was considered likely to be fatal, so the paper concluded that 'a cabin which may be jettisonable in an emergency appears to offer the most satisfactory solution'. The original HP80 cockpit had therefore to be redesigned and compressed with this in mind. Armoured protection was removed to save weight and a programme was initiated to produce $\frac{1}{15}$ scale dynamic models of the Avro and Handley Page bomber cabins with priority in testing being given to the HP80. The idea was that, in a serious emergency, the first pilot would press a button whereby the control linkages would sever and four explosive bolts would push the cabin capsule (including scanner bay) clear. Once free of the pitching fuselage, four hinged fins would stabilise the tumbling nose before a large parachute came out from behind to lower the capsule, with the crew still strapped in their 25g seats, gently to earth. The cabin relied on the collapse of the nose structure to absorb the shock of impact. It was a good way of getting the whole crew out quickly without hitting the recently added tail fin, but like many advanced ideas it was too complicated for the technology of the day. The Ministry also blew hot and cold as to whether it really wanted the thing anyway because of the development costs and time involved, but during the final phase of official enthusiasm in 1950 Handley Page acquired a quarter scale model of the nose from a sub-contractor and fitted it to the front of a 32ft span ML target glider. The stabilising fins and parachute were to be actuated automatically via 30ft of electric cable once the nose cleared the glider, but unfortunately the night before the trial a tidy-minded electrician found all this looped cable lying around and he shortened it. Consequently when the nose was fired off the following day, the cable snapped straight away; there being no power to operate the fins and parachute, the whole thing dropped like a stone.

An Avro Lincoln test vehicle was then sent to replace the glider but by then the Ministry had suffered an acute loss of interest, partially as a result of pressure from Avro which was getting nowhere with a jettisonable nose for their delta. The whole concept was therefore abandoned, leaving the HP80 nose to be fitted permanently to the fuselage by four large bolts where the explosive attachments were to have gone. All that remained of the idea was the plenum chamber, a partially pressurised compartment just behind the cockpit where the parachute was to have been stowed. It was subsequently extended by 42in to house most of the electrical connections to the cabin but in the beginning it was known at Radlett as 'Pilch's Attic' after the small humorous Cockney who was thin enough to squeeze inside and work there.

While a jettisonable nose was being investigated, the nose profile had been swept up with each pilot occupying a separate fighter-type blister canopy giving the HP80 a 'frog-eye' appearance. Then the nose was slightly swept down and a larger windscreen, flush with the fuselage streamlined shape, was fitted to keep down local shock waves and to give a very quiet cockpit while providing satisfactory vision for both pilots sitting side by side. Finally the cloud and collision warning scanner was deleted from the nose which was then extended to a sharp point to reduce kinetic heating.

Once the jettisonable nose was cancelled, Handley Page resurrected the proposal to fit ejection seats for all crew members. It would have been a major redesign problem to cut five jettisonable canopies in the pressure cabin roof yet it could have been done notwithstanding 'quite considerable' delays and extra costs. But the Ministry saw no justification for either, their philosophy now being that in the event of a mishap there would be sufficient time for the rear crew to make a free-fall exit. The pilots on the other hand would have taken longer to reach the exit door and there was a good chance that while they were so doing, the aircraft would become so unstable that escape would be difficult or impossible. Baling out manually from the roof risked impact with the fin or wing leading edge, so the pilots were to be provided with new 80ft/sec Martin-Baker ejection seats designed to clear the lofty tail.

The flightdeck was therefore altered once more to reposition the roof instrumentation and controls

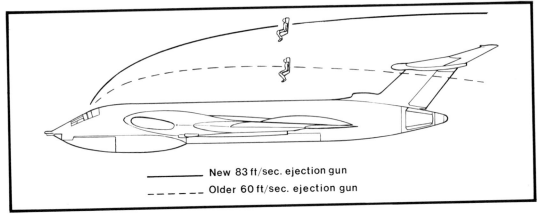

New 83 ft/sec. ejection gun

Older 60 ft/sec. ejection gun

to make way for the pilots' jettisonable canopies. The rear crew of three — for a sixth seat between front and back was fitted after November 1957 — now faced backwards in line abreast, and they were expected to bale out manually through the entry door on the port side which opened upwards and doubled as a windshielded emergency exit. It has to be said that this was a far from satisfactory arrangement. Test abandonments with 'aerodynamically representative dummies' in 1958 found that at speed in excess of 290kt, 'rear crew are likely to strike the intake lip when escaping', and human trials through the emergency exit were never attempted because they were 'too dangerous'. With hindsight, the RAF should have gone for ejection seats for all crew members from the beginning instead of wasting time on jettisonable cabins because, in opting for tomorrow's technology, they condemned HP80 rear crews to yesterday's.

The centre and rear fuselage were to all intents and purposes one component extending back to the fin leading edge. The main factor that rankled at Cricklewood throughout the war was the way the Halifax was always overshadowed by the Lancaster, which they ascribed to the fact that the Lancaster was capable of adaptation to carry far greater bomb loads and therefore always stole the limelight. Although the primary load of the advanced bomber was to be the first British atomic bomb, codenamed Blue Danube, Joy remembers that they strove to give their HP80 a bomb capacity double that of the Lancaster and in this endeavour they were greatly assisted by the crescent wing. Whereas the dimensions of the Valiant and the Avro delta bomb bays were somewhat restricted by great spars, the centre wing structure of the HP80 ended at about 30% chord and therefore,

because of the high sweep, the centre wing spar box was well forward of the aircraft's centre of gravity where it crossed the fuselage. This meant that the bomb bay had only to carry the weight of bombs or other military loads through four equally spaced fore and aft girders attached at intervals to heavy box-section frames. Two long bomb doors retracted inwards and were of double skin construction to give high torsional stiffness.

The inside the HP80 bomb bay was to be likened by the RAF to 'a poorly furnished railway carriage', but there was no denying its size. Back in 1947 the Specification had called for a total bomb capacity of 20,000lb made up of one Blue Danube, or two 10,000lb conventional bombs, or 18 1,000lb munitions. At the time it was thought that the nuclear weapon might be 6ft in diameter and up to 30ft long, and although Blue Danube eventually turned out to be much smaller than this, the initial stimulus resulted in a cavernous HP80 bomb bay some 5ft longer than that of the Avro 698. But more importantly for the honour of Handley Page, it had nearly twice the capacity. At a time when the Boeing B-52A bomber was being designed around a military load of 34,000lb, the HP80 despite being less than half the B-52's gross weight had a bomb bay theoretically big enough to accommodate, as an alternative to the bulky Blue Danube, one 22,000lb 'Grand Slam', two 12,000lb 'Tallboys', four 10,000lb bombs, or no fewer than

Above right:
The aircraft that kept Handley Page solvent while it wrestled with the Victor — the Hastings military transport. This version carried a H2S radar and was employed on No 1066 Flight to train Nav Radars for the V-force. The second Hastings prototype had a replica HP80 door inserted in the rear fuselage, and a representation of the Victor wing painted aft, for manual bale-out trials.

Right:
Blue Danube, the first British operational atomic bomb. The magnitude of the weapon which had to be fitted into the Victor bomb bay may be judged by the size of the Warrant Officer standing far right.

48 1,000lb bombs or 39 2,000lb Type 2 mines. All bomb loading was to be done by vehicle-mounted hydraulic jacks, making pits or ramps unnecessary; one 10,000lb bomb could be loaded in 10 minutes while a full load of 48 1,000lb bombs took only half an hour. 'It was another very important feature', said Godfrey Lee. 'There was so much that fitted together correctly in this aeroplane.'

Behind the bomb doors came a flash bomb bay. The RAF still clung to the World War 2 concept of target marking such that in November 1951, a pathfinder version of the HP80 was proposed to the Air Staff as the HP98. Structurally identical to the HP80, it was to be armed with remote-controlled radar-sighted tail guns for low altitude operations and powered by Rolls-Royce Conway 3 engines rated at 11,500lb static thrust plus 20% with water injection for take-off and short burst acceleration. The Air Staff declined the kind offer, ordering one prototype of the Valiant B2 instead, but in 1955 the RAF decided that they were never going to need Pathfinders of any sort in a nuclear war and the HP80's flash bomb bay was sealed up from the second prototype onwards.

Finally came the rear fuselage bulkhead in front of which was the rear equipment compartment. The bulkhead was designed to take the stress loads of the high T-type tail of similar construction to the wing, while right at the back were two large hydraulically operated clam-type airbrakes and stowage for the brake parachute. Under the fin was 'Annie's Room' which housed the air brake hydraulic selectors.

Below:
Fred's Shed in the early 1960s. This aircraft erection hall was 675ft long and 31ft high with an unobstructed width of 150ft. Each of the hall's five bays could be isolated by fire-resisting curtains, and three hardstandings outside the doors acted as extensions to the production line in fine weather. Aircraft moving through the hall are: far left, Hastings and Heralds; middle, Victor 2 with B1s behind; right, Victor 2 production line; far right, Hastings.
HP Association

The whole aeroplane was to be operated completely by irreversible flying controls. Handley Page considered incorporating manual reversion as on the Valiant but it rejected the idea because it would have needed two tremendous research and development programmes instead of one. Flying high and fast with shock waves all around it, the HP80 was expected to experience flutter problems associated with the high aspect ratio and relatively thin swept wings. Thus in Godfrey Lee's opinion, 'we didn't think we had a dog's chance of getting a manually controlled aircraft to meet that specification'.

H. M. Hobson of Wolverhampton supplied the electro-hydraulic power control units for the elevators, ailerons and rudders, and everyone agreed that the company did an excellent job. With no manual back-up, Stafford and Joy insisted on a duplicated system such that, for example, the port elevator could be operated irrespective of a complete failure on the starboard side and the aeroplane was still flyable even if one of the two remaining port sub-units failed. Although these powered flying control units had a very short life of around 90 flying hours at first, this was increased considerably in time and the units never once suffered a complete failure. Test pilots would always argue about elevator gearings and the right amount of 'artificial feel' that should be incorporated, but one of the great things about the HP80's controls in Ken Pratt's opinion was that 'from day one they stayed virtually as they were: it was very different from the time when we worked on manually controlled aircraft'.

The controls had many ingenious design features such as compact skew levers which converted linear into rotary motion without backlash or friction. Production aircraft were also to have a Mach trimmer to compensate for shifts in centre of pressure due to compressibility by automatically moving the elevators. The bomber later acquired electro-hydraulic yaw dampers on the rudder to cancel out 'Dutch roll' instability at height.

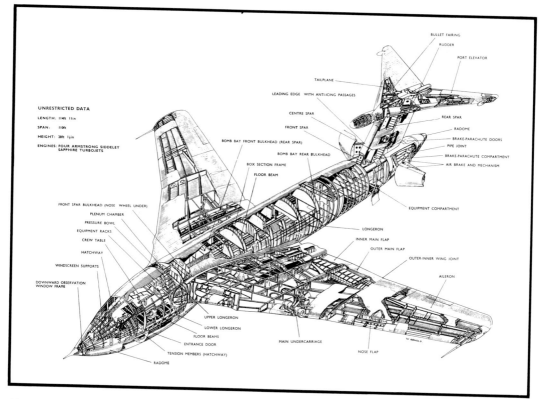

UNRESTRICTED DATA

LENGTH: 114ft 11in
SPAN: 110ft
HEIGHT: 28ft 1½in
ENGINES: FOUR ARMSTRONG SIDDELEY
SAPPHIRE TURBOJETS

Above:
Victor structure at a glance.

Powered flying control units, among a host of other services, were only possible because the HP80 was to be an all-electric aeroplane. The bomber's electrical system was designed by the Royal Aircraft Establishment but its installation in the HP80 — involving over 40 miles of cable — was the responsibility of two equally outspoken and excellent technicians, Peter Cronbach and then Sam Hall.

Prototype HP80 electrics were more akin to those of the Hermes IV but production aircraft relied on four free-running engine-driven 208V ac alternators converting to 112V dc through transformer-rectifiers. Direct current generators were not used because of brush wear problems at height, so the alternators had to go through the process of converting to dc because stored battery power was seen as essential to keep the powered flying controls working in the event of a total electrics failure.

However, although the electrics were simple, they were novel in-so-far as the port and starboard pairs of alternators fed separate busbars with essential electrical loads divided equally between

them. The bulky rectifier system was initially housed in the rear equipment compartment but once the jettisonable nose was scrapped, much useful space became available in the plenum chamber and all the circuit wizardry was moved up there.

How was a working bomber assembled from the 15,000 HP80 drawings and 40,000 detail parts? Up to the end of World War 2, Radlett had remained a flight shed operation where components manufactured at Cricklewood and elsewhere were put together into aircraft which were then flown out. Every year thereafter the firm intended to move entirely to Radlett but it was a slow transition which was not completed until 1965. Therefore, apart from component manufacture sub-contracted to the Woodley factory near Reading taken over by Handley Page in 1948 when Miles Aircraft Ltd went into liquidation, construction of the HP80 was split between Cricklewood and Radlett. Out of the same Cricklewood sheds that created the O/400 came detailed machine parts and stringers, sub-assemblies such as wing panels and fuselage frames, and much major sub-assembly work including the outer wings, fuselage tail cone, control surfaces and fin.

At Radlett, all non-HP80 work was relegated to the other side of the airfield leaving two establishments to deal with the new bomber. Park Street, at the northern end, was the research, development and experimental flying centre which by 1953 possessed a high speed wind tunnel fed by three Nene turbojets plus one of the largest structural test frames in the country. At the southern end was the Colney Street facility, devoted primarily to the manufacture of major sub-assemblies such as the front fuselage and flight deck, and final assembly of aircraft.

As production of the HP80 involved factories which were separated by 10 miles or so, a great deal of thought and planning went into ensuring that the bomber was comparatively easy to build. Handley Page had split the Halifax into major sections, each of which was suitable for production at small factories, and this was the key to the firm's gargantuan output of bombers during the war. Production of the HP80 was also geared, so far as was possible, to producing a large number of relatively small components instead of a small number of large ones. This made for less complicated jigs and tools, reduced to a minimum the time that any single component remained in a jig, and overcame the need to transport very big assemblies from Cricklewood to Radlett which saved time and cost. Not that some of the

components were all that small: one of the most remarkable machined components in the HP80 was the longeron running down the bomb bay which was the longest single unit in the structure at around 40ft.

Apart from production of sandwich panels in sub-assembly jigs before incorporation into major assembly structures, another 5,000 HP80 parts were stretch-formed. Complicated work such as construction of the wing spars was undertaken by Cricklewood's spar-milling machines. A normal vacuum moulding process was used to make the huge H2S scanner radome — layers of fibreglass and Hycar were built up and cured in large ovens to create the largest structure of its type yet made. Fibreglass was also used extensively for cable ducts.

Major and sub-assemblies produced at Cricklewood were then transported by road to Colney Street where they were mounted with Radlett parts in final assembly jigs prior to equipment installation. The various stages of final assembly began with the initial mating of 6ft thick inner wings with a 10ft diameter centre fuselage, and the whole process finished with the complete aircraft being ready to move to the paint shop and pre-flight hangar. It was said that five men skilled in all processes would spend their entire working lives building one HP80, so at a conservative estimate this represented 400,000 man-hours per production aircraft.

This then was 'Fred's Shed', a hive of activity geared to the cause of scientific simplification where a Victor would roll off the line every month. To the uninitiated, parts of the Handley Page factory resembled a massive covered market with work areas scattered about in apparent confusion. Yet out of it all, sophisticated aircraft emerged. Sir Frederick loved to recount the story of the USAF General who, after being shown round the HP80 production line declared, 'It's a great aircraft, but why do you have to build it in a barn?' But build it they did, and at the end of the day Sir Frederick concluded that his insistence on manufacturing economy had produced 'the best technical job which peace could afford'.

Right:
The Victor production line at Radlett showing the evolution from centre section to almost complete aircraft. *HP Association*

4
Victor Ludorum

'Open your gates and give the Victors way', wrote Shakespeare in *King John*, and in this spirit Sir Frederick hoped to get the first HP80 prototype airborne in March 1951 and thereafter sweep the field. But it was not to be. The target slipped to the Farnborough Show of 1952 and although in June of that year the company received an initial order for 25 HP80s, the Air Staff also ordered the same number of Avro 698s for comparative trials.

In the early days it was assumed that an order for 200-plus aircraft would go to one manufacturer, and as talk of comparative trials only reinforced this impression, the race was on to beat the 'northerners' — Avro was based in Manchester — into the air. Handley Page teams therefore worked all through the winter and spring of 1951/52 in the experimental shop trying to sort out all the usual development problems from silly things not fitting to whole systems having to be redesigned, all of which was compounded by the fact that no one had ever worked on such a massively sophisticated project before. Pre-flight testing of the powered controls, hydraulics and fuel system, which entailed stopping leaks, finding out where fluids had gone to and making them behave as they should, was, according to Ken Pratt, 'a nightmare story alone'. The Ministry did not help matters when, at the last moment, it declared Radlett airfield to be unsuitable for the maiden flight, so the first prototype had to be dismantled again and taken down to Boscombe Down where there was a 10,000ft runway with ample overshoot.

It is here that we come to the story of the good ship 'Geleypandhy'. A team of 60 Park Street men were detailed to reassemble the prototype at Boscombe, of which 14, led by their redoubtable Chief Engineer, William MacRostie, were to travel with the convoy. The 90-mile route to Boscombe had been carefully surveyed to determine all points where the fuselage might get stuck, and two critical T-junctions had been temporarily bypassed with the aid of bulldozers. The fuselage was mounted tail first on a suitably reinforced London Transport bus axle towed behind a powerful tractor coincidentally registered OHV 80. But the HP80 was to be no ordinary covered load. Some fertile brain in security decreed that it should be disguised, so the whole load was encased in white sheeting draped over a frame to resemble a ship's hull with the name 'GELEYPANDHY — SOUTHAMPTON' emblazoned on the side. Whether the anagram of Handley Page was misspelt on purpose we shall never know, but the 'flying boat' set off on 24 May along the North Circular Road and down the A30. It reached Andover after dawn only to find one of the T-junction by-pass cuttings blocked by the very bulldozer that had dug it. The bulldozer resisted all attempts to be started, so the track had to be widened with spades to allow the load to squeeze past. The HP80 got through to Boscombe unscathed but fate still decreed against an appearance at Farnborough that year. First came the discovery after reassembly that the centre of gravity was so far outside the permitted aft limit that it could only be balanced by ballasting the empty radar scanner bay with half a ton of scrap iron plates bolted under the flightdeck pressure floor. The second prototype was similarly 'modified' as it was too advanced to incorporate the eventual remedy of lengthening the fuselage by 42in. Then with only a month to go came tragedy. A high pressure hydraulic system operated the undercarriage, wheel brakes, main and nose flaps, bomb doors and airbrakes, and when the hydraulic system in the rear equipment compartment was being functionally tested, a fire broke out covering three fitters in burning hydraulic fluid. One of them, Eddie Eyles, died in hospital 16 days later.

Finally there were problems with the powered flying controls. They could only be tested on the completed airframe because the loads were so large, and all went well until the resonance checks which involved putting shocks into the control system to see if it could stand the strain. There were no problems with the rudders and ailerons but when the technicians thumped the elevators, the system self-excited itself so much that the noise was deafening. It took six weeks to find a cure.

By this time the prototype Avro 698 — shortly to be christened 'Vulcan' — had flown and the 1952 Farnborough Show had started, so much of

Above:
The V-bomber family showing off its distinctive aerodynamic shapes. Left to right are Vickers Valiant, Avro Vulcan and Victor. 'It may be asked why we have adopted three types instead of concentrating production on one', declared the Minister of Supply in 1952. 'My answer is that in equipping an air force it is, as in racing, risky to put all your money on one horse or try to spot the winner too long before the race.'

the impetus went out of getting the HP80 ready. As a small consolation the Park Street team went off to see the flying display, but they were so dog tired after their efforts that most fell asleep in the sun and got burnt. Maybe they stirred as the Vulcan showed off its paces overhead. It was left to Sir Frederick to keep the firm's end up by uttering, in the rich, mellow Cotswold accent that he retained to the end, apt biblical quotations about the superiority of they that cometh after.

The man who made ready to take the first HP80 prototype, WB771, into the air was Handley Page Chief Test Pilot, Sqn Ldr Hedley George Hazelden DFC and bar, RAF(Ret'd). Educated at Tonbridge, 'Hazel' had flown Hampdens and Lancasters during the war before attending the first course at the newly formed Empire Test Pilot's School in 1943. (Coincidentally, one of his instructors on that occasion was the man who first flew the Vulcan, Roly Falk.) Hazel had joined Handley Page in April 1947 at the age of 32, and within two months he was called into Chief Designer Stafford's office and told of the firm's latest challenge — a bomber they thought would be capable of 500kt, 50,000ft and a range of 5,000 miles. 'If you can find out how to build it', he told Reggie Stafford, 'I'll find out how to fly it.'

Hazel spent many hours after November 1950 learning to handle the Sapphire engines installed in place of the two outboard piston engines on the second Hastings prototype. He also flew a Sapphire-engined Canberra B2 to gain high speed engine handling experience, but he never had the opportunity to test the HP88.

'We could never be 100% certain that the first flight of the HP80 would be alright', said Godfrey Lee, 'but we had done all we could think of and had the backing from low and high speed wind tunnel tests, so we felt justified in putting old Hazel aboard and telling him to get on with it.' A week before Christmas 1952, WB771 was taxied for the first time; two days later Hazel began taxying on the main runway but he attempted nothing more adventurous because heavy rain restricted visibility. Then on 24 December, while the rest of the world was cranking up the Yuletide spirit, the skies cleared and the wind dropped to a light breeze. With flight test observer Ian Bennett, Hazel climbed aboard the silver HP80 and locked

Below:
The fuselage of the world's most advanced bomber, not so cunningly disguised as a ship's hull, sets out for the far-from-transonic 6½hr journey to Boscombe.
HP Association

Airborne at last — WB771 in its original silver grey finish early in 1953. The *Sunday Express* went so far as to say that the crescent wing was 'the greatest step forward in design in modern times'. *HP Association*

his radio on to transmit so that all he said could be heard on the ground. WB771, a flying shell weighing around 95,000lb, got airborne in less than 1,500ft of runway or one-quarter of the distance available at Radlett, which showed that someone had been over-cautious. Hazel then did two low circuits with the undercarriage down to test the ground effect of the combination of swept wing and high tail, before landing after a 17min flight. 'It was all so effortless', he said afterwards, 'it is difficult to see why we were so apprehensive.' He did not reveal that after landing he breathed a sigh of relief that was very audible in the Control Tower.

Nowadays a new aeroplane cannot be rolled out without the attendant glare of publicity, but in 1952 the first flight of a 'hush-hush' bomber was a very muted affair. Stafford had gone down to Boscombe with Hazel to keep the prototype company, while Joy and Lee remained at Cricklewood awaiting the call for a first flight that was on and then off every few days. Finally they received word that WB771 was really going to fly

that day, so they jumped into Joy's car and sped off. It is quite extraordinary to think that the main architects of such a revolutionary new aircraft might miss the climax of all their years of toil, but they were both afraid that they might be too late as they motored along. 'In the event', recalled Joy, 'we just got there in time. It was an ordinary Boscombe day with no undue security and we went across to the Control Tower and saw it take off and land, and that was the end of it. I think we had a drink in the Officers' Mess afterwards.'

The Goons were to give their own version of the HP80 story in their weekly BBC broadcast and on 2 January 1953 the Air Ministry officially announced that the aircraft had been named 'Victor'. It was said that it took 14 meetings of the Air Council to arrive at this decision but the new name completed the trio of V-bomber types and gave much pleasure in passing to Gustav Victor Lachmann. Aircraft handling trials continued successfully at Boscombe for two months while the Radlett runway was extended northwards to make it officially suitable for flight testing of production aircraft. Nevertheless on the fourth flight on 3 February, during which the undercarriage was raised and lowered, all 16 tyres burst on landing because of a malfunctioning interlock between the parking brake and retraction button. Towards the end of its stay at Boscombe, Hazel overflew Radlett to show off the Victor to the workforce who had built it, and on 24 February WB771 returned home to the new 6,910ft runway. It was at Radlett during a heavy landing shortly afterwards that the port undercarriage bogie skipped and jammed at an angle, but Hazel made a successful delicate recovery on eight starboard wheels and four rear tyres on the port.

The Victor prototype made its official public debut over Odiham on 15 July during the Queen's Coronation Review flypast, and a week later ACM Sir John Baker, the Controller of Aircraft, was taken up for a ride; Sir John was very impressed with the bomber's manoeuvrability but he found the pilots' view somewhat restricted. Other notables followed suit including the Secretary of the USAF, Harold E. Talbot. 'Flying this ship is just as easy as a baby carriage', he declared afterwards to a bemused audience, none of whom had ever previously likened the Victor to a pram, but he was probably referring to Hazel's party trick of landing the Victor 'hands off'. Stafford had

predicted before the maiden flight that the aircraft would land itself because, whereas most aircraft have to be 'held off' just before touchdown to counter the nose-down moment caused by rising ground killing the tail downwash, the Victor was not so affected because its tailplane was high and half the normal size. In addition its swept wing produced induced downwash at the roots and upwash at the tips, which made the nose ease up of its own accord as the wings neared the ground. So the nose-up moment from the wing more than compensated for the nose-down effect from the tail — 'Get it properly set up on the approach', said Hazel, 'and I promise you it will make a perfect landing if you just leave it alone.' His concluding words — 'at this rate we shall soon be out of work and only passengers and bombs will fly' — were not to be realised because the Victor's self-landing qualities largely disappeared when Handley Page shortened the tail and dispensed with the nose flaps. Boscombe Down test pilots were also to dismiss the self-landing characteristic as 'of no particular advantage'.

At the end of August WB771 went into the Radlett paint shop to be decked out in an eerie matt black finish with red fuselage trimmings and silver-grey wings and tail for the 1953 Farnborough Show. Over 30 years later it is difficult to

Below:
WB771 in its element. The hole in the dorsal fillet at the base of the fin provided air for transformer-rectifier cooling and for anti-icing.

appreciate the impact of colourful new types such as the Victor on the national consciousness. The glorious Coronation and the conquest of Everest epitomised the final leap out of the slough of postwar rationing and uncertainty, and the black-hulled Victor sitting on its bogies 'like a science-fiction spaceship awaiting setting up for launching' was acclaimed with pride as a guardian of the new Elizabethan age. Hazel's demonstration at Farnborough, made entirely on three engines due to a last-minute failure, did nothing but enhance the enthusiasm of the occasion.

The V-bombers were the first British aircraft to be treated as 'weapons systems', their respective manufacturers being given complete responsibility for melding the airframes, engines and avionics into a composite whole. Bob Hayes was Project Engineer on the Victor from 1948-55 and some indication of the complexity of the jigsaw he had to fit together can be gained from the fact that the Victor carried 60 times the weight of radio and electronic equipment of the Halifax.

The Handley Page flight test department which proved and tested every system never had more than three test pilots on its staff, though Sqn Ldr Baldwin and then Sqn Ldr Ringer were later detached to Radlett as RAF liaison pilots. An average test flight crew consisted of a pilot in the left-hand seat, a flight observer in the co-pilot's seat, and another observer down the back to monitor the electrics and instrumentation. Hazel generally earned his £1,300 a year salary by climbing WB771 out from Radlett towards East Anglia before flying up and down the coast. Test pilots needed free air in which to operate and as the recently introduced civil airways system stopped at 25,000ft, WB771 had the skies to itself when Hazel took it up to 50,000ft for the first time on 15 October 1953. Thereafter the Victor prototype made good progress, and in the era of the DC-6 it was a pretty impressive sight as it came in to land with everything out and down. Several times it flew two or three trials a day, and once four.

Mach 0.88 was reached on 3 November and a few days later Hazel clocked up Mach 0.91 at 47,500ft. The prototype's Sapphire 6 engines had been down-rated to 7,500lb thrust for the initial flights but they were back up to their 8,300lb design rating by the time WB771 had amassed 50hr flying time at the end of the year. On the last day of December excessive engine vibration made the starboard inner flap drop off during a system check. With no apparent increase in drag, Hazel did not appreciate the loss until after landing, thereby demonstrating what successive generations of pilots were to discover — that the Victor was under-flapped. The missing flap made a solo touchdown in a garden in Chorleywood.

Above:
WB771 lifts off at Farnborough in 1953 in the new red and black colour scheme personally chosen by Sir Frederick. The lowered leading edge flaps are prominent and the main undercarriage bogies are in the trail position prior to retraction. *Quadrant/Flight*

The prototype was steep-turning at Mach 0.88 without buffet by 5 February 1954, and at the end of the month Hazel reached Mach 0.925 at 45,000ft with no compressibility effects other than an easily held nose-down trim change between Mach 0.90 and 0.91. At this stage WB771 had logged 60hr but then it was inadvertently flown at Mach 0.98 which strained the tailplane causing slight permanent skin buckling. The aircraft was therefore grounded

Below:
Back home to Radlett. 'I must say how pleased I was to read and hear about your new long range bomber', wrote Lord Trenchard to Sir Frederick. 'I would very much like to have a fly in it one day, if I may.' Unfortunately Lord Trenchard died in 1956 before his wish could be fulfilled. *HP Association*

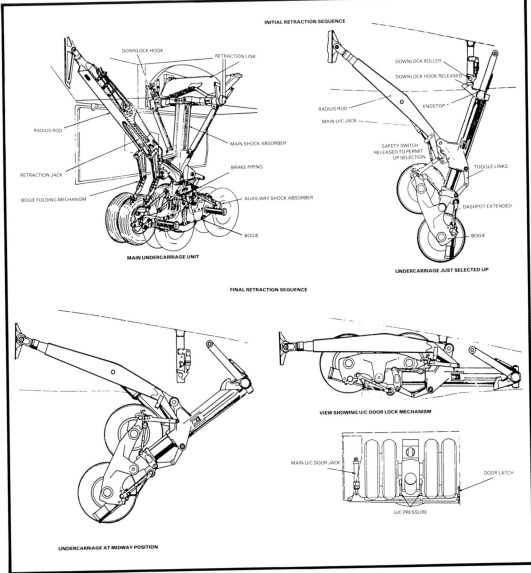

INITIAL RETRACTION SEQUENCE

DOWNLOCK HOOK

RETRACTION LINK

DOWNLOCK ROLLER

DOWNLOCK HOOK RELEASED

RADIUS ROD

MAIN U/C JACK

ENDSTOP

RADIUS ROD

RETRACTION JACK

MAIN SHOCK ABSORBER

BRAKE PIPING

BOGIE FOLDING MECHANISM

AUXILIARY SHOCK ABSORBER

SAFETY SWITCH
RELEASED TO PERMIT
UP SELECTION

TOGGLE LINKS

DASHPOT EXTENDED

BOGIE

BOGIE

MAIN UNDERCARRIAGE UNIT

UNDERCARRIAGE JUST SELECTED UP

FINAL RETRACTION SEQUENCE

VIEW SHOWING U/C DOOR LOCK MECHANISM

MAIN U/C DOOR JACK

DOOR LATCH

U/C PRESSURE

UNDERCARRIAGE AT MIDWAY POSITION

for a thorough inspection and the tailplane was replaced with one borrowed from the second prototype. At the same time modifications were made to the throttle controls, and the aileron rate was enhanced to counter a tendency to roll to port after take-off.

WB771 returned to the air on 14 June and after a further 24hr flying it began a series of airspeed calibration flights at Cranfield. All went well until 14 July when Hazel was to have flown the Victor in the morning before driving across to Woodley in the afternoon to test fly a Marathon for the benefit of a Japanese admiral. At the last moment he received a phone call to say that the admiral had arrived early, and he remembers looking across his desk at Ronald 'Taffy' Ecclestone who had only recently arrived as an assistant test pilot. Taffy was grinning at Hazel and saying that he would fly the Victor to let his Chief get across to Reading, so Hazel gave him a full brief and went off.

Air speed indicator pressure error tests involved flying at low level past a camera mounted on top of a Cranfield hangar to enable observers to measure the height of the aircraft accurately above the known camera site and to calculate the barometric pressure differential between the two positions. It was a task best suited to the calm of dusk or dawn but even though Ecclestone flew by again and again at faster and faster speeds — air speed indicators have different pressure errors at different speeds — no one would have expected the whole tailplane to come away from the fin as it did. Taffy Ecclestone and his crew did not stand a chance even though WB771 did carry on flying momentarily before crashing in a pall of black smoke at the intersection of the Cranfield runways.

The accident was caused by tail flutter cracking the bolt holes in the fin, allowing the three bolts securing the tailplane to loosen and shear in quick succession. Tail dihedral was the fatal flaw but although the firm had appreciated the risks from the start, the fates had conspired to obscure its effect on the tail/fin joint. For a start Handley Page made a low-speed wind tunnel flutter model which proclaimed that the flutter speed was acceptable, but someone in the stress office miscalculated the stiffness of the tail/fin attachment which was more flexible than that represented on the model. Then the flutter speeds were calculated from resonance test results which incorporated the right degree of stiffness, but the mistake made here was of not allowing for the dihedral effect which meant that as the tailplane yawed it had a bit of rolling moment as well. It was careless but again it produced a safe answer. Finally, rudder kicks were administered in flight to monitor dampings but no one realised that there were two frequencies very close together; while one was well damped, the other, which was not damped and was the fatal one, went unnoticed. So three independent tests all gave the same safe answer yet they were all wrong. 'Well, it happens', said Godfrey Lee resignedly. It was obvious to Lee after the accident that if they had taken the dihedral off and put a bigger fin on, the misfortune would not have happened, 'but it seemed like getting something for nothing and we did not know what a killer we'd built in'. The cure was to reduce local stress concentration by spreading the load over four bolts and by stiffening production fins. Even so, getting the right degree of stiffness was still a matter of trial and error, and test pilot Jock Still did some of the best flutter tests ever made when he took the second prototype to within 15kt of destruction to prove that tunnel results on an intermediate stage of fin stiffening were wrong.

Using a repaired version of WB771's original tailplane, the second prototype, WB775, was completed as quickly as possible in the same black and silver-grey livery as its predecessor. The Resident Technical Officer allowed it to make a 57min maiden flight on 11 September without main undercarriage doors so that it could qualify to appear in the 1954 Farnborough flypast that same afternoon.

On 1 February 1955 the Victor bomb doors were opened in flight for the first time and resulting buffet was within acceptable limits. The flash bomb compartment doors were also fully opened a month later, but the flash bomb requirement was cancelled on 30 June and these doors were deleted from production aircraft by Modification No 50 and permanently sealed thereafter on WB775.

On completion of the company's own trials, Handley Page delivered WB775 to the Aeroplane

Left:
Model of the Victor tail under structural test at Radlett. The whole aircraft was tested on a specially reinforced concrete floor with loads being applied in uniform increments. Most test cases were taken to between 85-90% of design ultimate conditions.
HP Association

& Armament Experimental Establishment (A&AEE) at Boscombe Down on 14 March. A&AEE would be ultimately responsible for clearing the Victor into RAF service so Handley Page thought it prudent to loan the second prototype to Boscombe for two weeks for a preview assessment. Although WB775 was restricted to 248kt at low level in the wake of the Cranfield accident, three A&AEE test pilots concluded after 14½hr flying that 'the aircraft was easy and pleasant to fly and appeared to have a high potential as a bomber aircraft'. Various aspects of the cockpit layout were regarded as unsatisfactory, especially crew comfort and field of view. 'However, particularly commendable features were the light and effective controls, the aircraft's response to control movement, the excellent infinitely variable airbrakes and the small changes of trim with speed and change in configuration.' After a satisfactory night flying assessment, WB775 went to Orfordness for bombing trials in June but thereafter the second prototype faded into the background as the production Victors started to roll off the line.

The first 25 production Victor B1s were ordered in June 1952 and the production specification, B128P, was agreed at a Cricklewood design conference on 22 August. A total of £3½ million had already been paid for the two prototypes and associated test specimens, and the price of the first 25 production Victors (XA917-XA941) was finally agreed at £450,000 per aircraft. Nevertheless, this

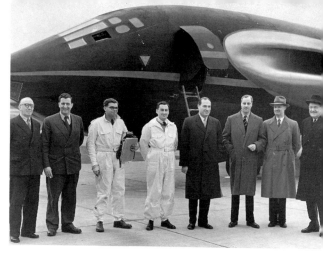

Above:
Handley Page notables in front of their pride and joy. Left to right are W. H. MacRostie (Chief Engineer), Hazel, Bob Williams (Senior Flight Observer who was later to die when the Mk 2 prototype crashed at St Bride's Bay), Johnny Allam, Air Cdre Arthur Vere Harvey MP (Chairman of the Conservative Party Air & Civil Aviation Committee and an HP director), Gp Capt The Hon George Ward MP (Under Secretary of State for Air), Reggie Stafford and Sir Frederick. This picture was taken before the two MPs went for a flight in the Victor.

sum did not include the cost of embodiment loan items such as the engines, and there were some 2,200 items of equipment in the Victor supplied on embodiment loan or by outside manufacturers.

There were not many noticeable differences between the prototypes and production Victor B1s. Apart from additional windows in the cockpit roof to improve field of view, 42in had to be added to the production plenum chamber to move the centre of gravity forward (moving the electrics into the plenum chamber also helped) and to give the crew a fighting chance of baling out successfully by moving the door away from the port engine intake. Production Victor fins were also shortened by 15in to reduce flexural resonance following the Cranfield accident. At the same time, the 'acorn' at the

Below:
The second prototype, WB775, at Radlett in March 1955.

junction of the fin and tailplane was revised and the dorsal fillet and equipment-cooling air intake were removed from the base of the fin, only the anti-icing air intake remained.

After many years of preoccupation with smooth surface finish, Handley Page then became very concerned about drag lines and the establishment of buffet boundaries during flight trials. To prevent early buffet and hence loss of aerodynamic efficiency, the Victor began to sprout the latest in aeronautical fashion, vortex generators. Twenty-three of these small vanes were fitted to each wing from the tip to just inboard of the nose flaps, and they stuck out vertically into the airflow to keep it attached to the wing by inducing rotating vortices to re-energise the boundary layer. The airbrakes also grew 'horns'. Handley Page designed some lovely tail airbrakes but initially they were more decorative than efficient so strakes had to be added to the top and bottom to produce more drag. These modified brakes caused no pitch-up whatsoever but they were now so good at breaking up the airflow that they caused problems for the relatively fragile tail cone behind.

At the end of this cone came the latest modification to the Victor brake parachute. The original intention was to fit a single 13ft Gregory-Quilter tail arrestor chute for emergencies or when landing on short runways, but when WB771 trials proved this to be inadequate, it was decided to fit four 8ft diameter chutes instead. When frequent failures of the 8ft chutes used up two or three at a time, a single but larger

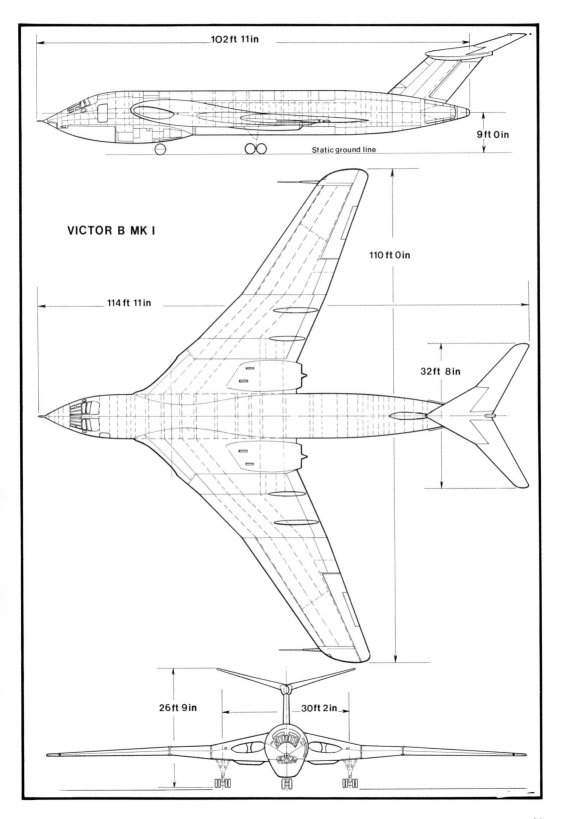

102 ft 11 in

9 ft 0 in

Static ground line

VICTOR B MK I

110 ft 0 in

114 ft 11 in

32 ft 8 in

26 ft 9 in

30 ft 2 in

Above:
Sideview of XA917. Notice the additional cockpit panels above the windscreen which were added on production aircraft to improve the view from the flightdeck.

Below:
XA918 lands in March 1956. At this stage the aircraft was still fitted with four small GQ brake parachutes.
Quadrant/Flight

Gregory-Quilter arrestor chute was fitted again after 1955.

The first production Victor B1, XA917, took to the air on 1 February 1956. Dressed overall in matt silver with big black serial numbers, XA917 stayed airborne for 15min at the hands of Johnny Allam, one-time RAF flying instructor, personal pilot to AM Sir Richard Atcherley, and graduate of both the Empire and US Naval Test Pilots Schools. Powered by Sapphire Sa7 Mk202 engines rated at 11,000lb, XA917 was no sluggard and on 1 June 1957 it became the largest aircraft in the world to break the sound barrier. On a test flight from Gaydon in Warwickshire, Johnny Allam put XA917 into a shallow dive at 40,000ft, 'inadvertently' failed to keep an eye on the machmeter, and clocked up 675mph which represented Mach 1.02 — the double sonic bang was heard from Banbury to Watford. The Victor was quite stable throughout giving observer Paul Langston little sensation of what was going on; he landed with the distinction of being the first man to break the sound barrier going backwards.

XA917 never entered RAF service because the first five production Victors were allotted for acceptance and operational trials extending over nine months: XA917 eventually crash-landed at Radlett after nearly 500hr of trials flying and its nose now houses the crew-drill trainer at RAF Marham. XA918 first flew on 21 March 1956 but XA919 was reserved as the 'conference' airframe and it did not fly until 13 March 1957. By the time the Minister of Supply, Reginald Maudling, officially opened the new 675ft long final assembly hall at Radlett on 26 March 1957, XA920 and XA921 were nearing completion.

The four aircraft up to XA920 sported the standard RAF lightweight aluminium finish — XA920 flew on 12 May — but from XA921 onwards Victors were coated in Titanine all-white anti-flash paint designed to reflect the intense heat-flash radiated by a nuclear explosion. XA921 was first flown on 20 June and a month later it flew to Marham to act as a static exhibit for the Queen's Review of Bomber Command on 23 July. Such was the might of Bomber Command in those days that three Victors and three Vulcans flew past in mass formation behind 18 Valiants and 72 Canberras.

The Victor performed many feats that belied its size in those early days besides going supersonic. Johnny Allam did slow rolls, loops and rolls-off-the-top at Farnborough before Hazel put a stop to

Below:
The first production Victor, in its matt silver finish, flies alongside a Victor car for a Vauxhall publicity photograph. The next time you see a Saab advert doing likewise, remember that the British thought of the idea first. *National Motor Museum*

what was becoming a rivet-popping contest with the Vulcan. Not that Hazel was averse to pushing the Victor to its limits at times — on maximum rate descent trials he throttled back at 50,000ft, did a wing over, opened the airbrakes and hurtled down at maximum speed to reach 3,000ft in just over 3min. A standard Handley Page test pilot's trick was to approach Radlett at 6,000ft, wait until the runway threshold had passed under the nose, then close the throttle, open the airbrakes and land with concrete to spare. It was great stuff, helped by the fact that there never was such an aircraft as the Victor with a comparable array of stall warnings. The first indication was the illumination of the coefficient of lift lights accompanied by automatic lowering of the nose flaps, provided they were selected to AUTO. Around this speed some peculiar noises — likened to an elephant trumpeting — emanated from the nostril air intakes as the flow broke down. Buffeting started perceptibly some 30-40kt below the flap-operating speed, increasing in violence down to the stall proper. Yet as soon as the back-pressure was released, the aircraft jumped out. 'No one could possibly inadvertently stall a Victor', said Hazel.

Being a big, strong chap, Hazel never worried about control forces. Handley Page's Chief Test

Pilot had a reputation for believing that any pilot who could not hold a 100lb control column load with one hand was a cissy, and he is jokingly blamed for the fact that so many Handley Page aircraft were heavy to fly. However, the reason why the Victor had a spectacle control column, unlike the fighter-type stick on the Vulcan, was because Hazel always adhered to the view that the forces on an aircraft's controls ought to reflect to the pilot the sort of aeroplane he was flying. He did not believe that heavy aircraft should be designed with controls as light as those of a Spitfire, despite the introduction of artificial feel which allowed

designers to impose whatever response they liked within the limits of the powered flying control motors. Even so, the RAF was to decide that the Victor controls were too light and Handley Page had to heavy them all up.

There were 10 production Victor B1s in existence by the time XA927 got airborne on 29 December 1956 but their introduction into front line service was delayed pending completion of retrospective modifications and the fitment of operational equipment. Thus the first Victor was not officially delivered to the RAF until No 232 Operational Conversion Unit (OCU) received the

15th production aircraft, XA931, on 28 November 1957. Based at Gaydon, 232 OCU had existed since February 1955 with Valiants divided between its two autonomous 'A' and 'B' Squadrons. Then in December 1956, 'A' Squadron disbanded while its instructors converted on to the Victor at Radlett. The Squadron officially re-formed at Gaydon on 28 November 1957 under Sqn Ldr Tony Ringer, and thereafter 'A' Squadron was responsible for converting RAF crews to the Victor B1 while 'B' Squadron looked after Valiant training.

XA931 was quickly followed by XA932, XA933, XA934 and, a little later, XA926. Early in 1958, XA923-XA925 were equipped at Park Street with 'Yellow Aster' reconnaissance radar before being attached to No 232 OCU to help train Valiant reconnaissance crews bound for No 543 Squadron at Wyton. When this was complete in April, the Yellow Aster trio broke away from the OCU to form the Radar Reconnaissance Flight at Wyton where they were joined by XA935. This was a time when reconnaissance had as high a priority as bombing.

Turning to bombing, by 1 April 1958 sufficient crews had passed out of No 232 OCU to re-form No 10 Squadron at Cottesmore, Rutland; the Squadron became operational when it received its first Victor, XA927, on 15 April. In June, 'A' Squadron of No 232 OCU carried out 1,000hr intensive flying trials to prove that the Victor could operate under pressure, and when these were completed in August the aircraft structure was checked. Tail attachment points came under particular scrutiny and a crack was found in a tailplane member, but the cause was traced to overtightening during assembly; construction procedures were altered but all Victors were grounded for a fortnight while their tailplanes were removed and replaced.

It had taken 11 years from the issue of Spec B35/46 to the establishment of the first Victor bomber squadron, and this fell far short of the target date set at the 1952 design conference which aimed for first delivery in March 1955 followed by the remaining 24 of the first contract by March 1957. For the defence it must be said that the Victor was the most sophisticated of all the V-bombers and Handley Page was such a relatively small firm that it was to be congratulated on getting near the target at all. At the height of design work on the HP80, the total number of engineers and technicians numbered barely 150. As the total Handley Page workforce numbered just around 5,000 — less than the design and engineering staffs alone at Boeing across the Atlantic — with not a great deal of work subcontracted outside, it is not surprising that the Victor took as long as it did to enter service. Yet in spite of the expert view that Handley Page had about one-quarter of the personnel that the Victor programme really needed, there was never a moment in Charles Joy's opinion 'when we did not think it was within our grasp'.

When Mr Beswick MP asked when the first Victor Squadron was to be formed in a Parliamentary Question on 30 May 1956, the Secretary of State for Air replied that the Victor's entry into service was delayed mainly by development difficulties and the crash of the first prototype. He also mentioned a strike in the Handley Page drawing office which held up work for four months, plus more recent trouble with the Sapphire 7 turbine blades which restricted engine life to 50hr and thereby hampered the flight test programme. But it must also be remembered that the design, manufacture and trials of the avionics inside the Victor were just as much exercises to the

Below:
The No 232 OCU crew who collected the unit's first Victor from Handley Page is seen here at Radlett before the historic delivery flight. Left to right are Sqn Ldr Tony Ringer AFC (Captain), Sqn Ldr K. W. Rogers (Co-pilot), Sqn Ldr P. J. Evans (Nav Plotter), Flt Lt J. E. Walton (Nav Radar, though he was called a 'bomb aimer' in 1957) and Flt Lt Harry Glendenning (AEO).

Above left:
XA931, the first Victor to enter operational service, arrives at Gaydon on 28 November 1957. It is finished in the new all-white anti-flash Titanine paint scheme which added 173lb to the weight of the average bomber because the thick paint absorbed heat by melting. *Quadrant/Flight*

Left:
XA917 at Farnborough in 1957. By now small perspex rain deflectors had been fitted just ahead of the long glass cockpit panels. *Quadrant/Flight*

edge of contemporary technology as the bomber itself. The Operational Requirement for the H2S Mk9A radar for instance was only issued in September 1948 and during 1957 Victors were stockpiling at Radlett pending arrival and fitment of the bombing and navigation systems.

Nor did the RAF help matters when it kept moving the goal posts. For example there had been complete agreement on Victor cockpit layout at the 1952 design conference, yet Boscombe test crews were particularly scathing about this aspect when they made their flight assessment of the second prototype in March 1955:

'The overall layout of the cockpit fell far short of the standard required in this class of aircraft. Generally, there appeared to be no logical grouping of associated controls and indicators and in certain aspects the layout was haphazard. The layout of the power control switch panel was illogical and dangerous. Some of the indicators and controls for primary services could only be operated by the first pilot, and several warning and monitoring devices were not visible to both pilots, making it impossible for either pilot to relax completely at any time. The extreme discomfort of the pilots' stations was severely criticised and will result in a lowering of efficiency and morale during only average length sorties.

'In conditions of poor visibility the restricted view was inadequate for the circuit and landing, and concern was felt for possible external windscreen reflections during night flying. It is essential that these major criticisms be rectified before the aircraft can be considered acceptable for Service use.'

The only answer to a blast such as this was for Handley Page to completely redesign the flight-deck which again took time.

Could the Victor have been brought into service quicker if it had been ordered in bigger numbers earlier? Certainly the firm had need of a decent-sized order and it had little to show for the effort and production facilities expended on the advanced bomber when Sir Frederick told his shareholders in 1953 that it was regrettable that 'big programmes' could not be ordered into production straight away so that a manufacturer could buy in bulk and achieve economies of scale. Handley Page was building so little in the early 1950s — the last Hastings had been completed and the Hermes was losing money — that the firm subcontracted for 150 Canberras ordered as part of the Korean War expansion programme. Although half this order was cancelled in 1953 to cope with the first Victor contract, a year later Sir Frederick was still calling for 'efficient, mechanised, mass production' of the Victor. Yet even though the

bomber was eventually added to the list of aircraft enjoying 'super-priority' status, this grandiose designation meant little in reality because no fewer than 11 other projects were equally blessed.

As far as Charles Joy was concerned, 'super-priority' did no more than get his firm at the head of the queue for precious raw materials and scarce forging capacity, and therefore 'it only helped us to produce the number of aircraft we said we were going to build, not more'. Even if hundreds of Victors had been ordered in the early 1950s, most could not have been made before the end of the decade by which time the nation would have been saddled with hosts of B1s when it would have preferred the improved B2 version. 'People were working as hard as they could to meet the requirements of the Specification anyway', said Ken Pratt; in Reggie Stafford's opinion, 'it was one of the few cases where a bigger order to start with would have made no difference'.

How did the Victor compare with its arch rival, the Vulcan? The Victor had a greater range and ceiling because of its better maximum lift coefficient and lower drag — Lee calculated that the original Avro 698 wing had about 120% of the transonic drag of the crescent — but low wing loading was the key to the Vulcan's superior manoeuvrability and take-off performance. The Victor was the more sophisticated design of the pair especially when it came to systems, but this was not necessarily a good thing. Handley Page's split busbar electrics were way ahead of their time and the Vulcan B1 had nothing like the same degree of electrical redundancy in the air. But the Victor hydraulics, which involved separate circuits to the different services, operated with a will of their own in the early days. Handley Page men were forced to admit that they added to their troubles by striving to make the Victor more sophisticated than it need have been.

Lift devices were a case in point. At one time or another the HP80 was to have had leading edge slats, nose flaps on the underside of the elevators, and contraflaps between the flaps and ailerons. Contraflaps were one of Stafford's contributions to the Victor, being an anti-pitch-up device pioneered by the Germans, and both contraflaps and elevator nose flaps were fitted to the first prototype as a contingency measure. In the event they remained locked up because flight trials proved them to be unnecessary.

The Vulcan's simpler systems generally proved to be just as efficient in the end, and the delta managed to compensate for the Victor's theoretically higher ceiling by carrying more powerful engines. The production Victor B1 never graduated beyond Sapphire 7 engines with a maximum thrust of 11,000lb, which made it underpowered in comparison with the Vulcan B1 which carried

13,500lb Olympus engines by 1958. But if we compare like for like in 1955, the Victor had the edge. Its shape remained virtually the same from 1948 right through to production, while Avro had to redesign their Vulcan wing in 1949 when RAE proved that bringing the line of maximum thickness sharply forward avoided the loss of effective sweep inboard. Lee already had known this because he had discussed the very topic with Ludwieg at Göttingen in 1945. Furthermore Avro had to put a kink in the Vulcan wing to increase buffet threshold after the first prototype had flown. The fact that Avro was forced to turn their Vulcan into what amounted to a crescent-delta as late as 1955 speaks volumes for the firm foundation on which the Victor was built.

Handley Page and Avro always thought there would be a final fly-off to choose between them, and their comments on each other's creation were sometimes amusing — 'What's that, an aeroplane?' 'What's that, a fish?' When the Victor was named, the Avro house journal went so far as to comment that 'it can only be a matter of time before the aircraft becomes known as the Vanquished'. But such banter was rare because of the fierce rivalry between the two companies

which, in Reggie Stafford's opinion, 'started right at the top'. The antagonism between Sir Frederick and his opposite number in Manchester, Sir Roy Dobson, was very real indeed. A typical example of the war of nerves occurred at the Odiham Coronation Review in June 1953 when WB771 was booked to fly past at 288kt. Sir Roy Dobson managed to get '460kt' printed in the official programme alongside the prototype Vulcan entry even though it is doubtful if the delta had been cleared to such a speed or could even reach it on the thrust of its interim 6,500lb engines.

All of which might seem childish with hindsight but both Sir Roy and Sir Frederick were both firm supporters of competition and Avro's Chief Designer recounted that 'our competitors at Handley Page provided a far more powerful spur than the exhortations of the Ministry of Supply'. In the end though, there were no losers because the Ministry took the line of least resistance and ordered both Victor and Vulcan into mass production.

Below:
Eight Victor B1s of No 10 Squadron are pictured lined up at their Cottesmore base in 1958.

5
Bigger and Better

The Victor was officially Released to Service in July 1957 during a series of proving tests conducted by the A&AEE at Boscombe between January 1957 and March 1958. The first four production aircraft were all involved but the main test Victor was XA920 which incorporated a Mach trimmer, yaw damper, automatic nose flap system and improved cockpit.

A&AEE test crews considered that the handling qualities of the Victor B1 'are in all respects adequate for its role and are in many aspects commendable. With all stability aids functioning, the aircraft is generally easy and pleasant to fly and it should be well liked by Service crews'. However, Boscombe found the Victor to be underpowered and noted that 'further structural development is urgently required to increase the maximum permitted airspeed to give a margin over the optimum climbing speed, to increase the maximum weight to permit the carriage of full fuel with normal bomb load, and to achieve the design values of normal acceleration'. The report concluded that the lift available before the onset of buffet was sufficient to permit a significant increase in cruising altitude but that the Victor B1's performance to date 'may soon be inadequate for a bomber operating against an integrated defence system'.

The Victor was therefore released 'for use in the RAF by day or night in temperate climates only' with a maximum permissible take-off and emergency landing weight of 160,000lb and a maximum speed of 330kt. To increase climb speed to 360kt and to be capable of greater heights or ranges, the Victor needed to be improved, and quickly.

The question was how to achieve this in a cost-effective manner. Back in 1952, the Operational Requirements Branch had tentatively asked Handley Page to consider 'the use of rocket boost for increasing altitude for short periods during cruise on the HP80 at 160,000lb take-off weight with 10,000lb of bombs'. Charles Joy reported back on 19 August that preliminary assessments showed it would be feasible to boost the bomber up from 50,000ft to 60,000ft in a few seconds if an attack was imminent: the only drawback was that the weight penalty of carrying

both rockets and rocket fuel would reduce overall range by 'up to 2,300 miles'. So died a rather impractical scheme, and it only highlighted the inherent contradiction between a customer which wanted the best of all worlds and a manufacturer which had so far only received an order for 25 Victors and which desperately needed a further contract to keep the wolf from its door rather than yet more changes to the specification.

In March 1955 Handley Page submitted price tenders for either 33 or 50 extra Victors to supplement the first 25. The Ministry's initial response was to order a further 25 Victors and 39 Vulcans, but Sir Frederick made such a fuss that in May 1955 he was rewarded with a contract for 33 more Victors at the reduced price of £244,000 apiece.

Handley Page would have preferred to claw back some of its research and development costs by continuing the run of Victor B1s, but the Air Staff wanted more height over target as quickly as possible. 1955 saw the erection of the first Soviet surface-to-air missile (SAM) battery around Moscow, and the RAF was looking towards more potent Victors to keep out of trouble. The Ministry saw them being powered initially by 14,000lb thrust Sapphire 9 engines, then being developed for the thin-winged Javelin fighter, inside a new Victor wing span of 115ft; in time it was hoped to see Conway or Olympus engines in a new centre section giving a total wing span of 137ft. These projections were known as Phase 2 and Phase 3 developments respectively, and Ministry studies showed that with Olympus or Conway engines the Victor would gain 8,000-10,000ft in ceiling while carrying a heavier load further.

When Reggie Stafford looked into the proposals, he concluded that Phase 3 — which was classified as the HP104 because it was virtually a new design — would come to fruition more quickly if six Sapphire 9s were used in place of the Conways which he did not regard as a paying proposition without much more development. The firm was convinced that the Victor only needed more thrust to fly higher and on the eve of the 1955 Farnborough Show, Sir Frederick chided Lord Hives of Rolls-Royce that the Conway's performance to date was not good enough to do justice to the Victor airframe and that this was the chief reason for the Ministry's reticence in placing further follow-on orders.

At the end of September Stafford discussed the relative merits of the Conway and Olympus with AVM Satterley, Assistant Chief of Air Staff (Operational Requirements). The Air Staff still had doubts about Rolls-Royce's claims for the Conway and they preferred a Victor Phase 3 with either four Olympus or six Sapphire 9s. Knowing that this would necessitate a rebuild because of the drastically revised centre-section involved, yet appreciating that the Government wanted to encourage development of the Conway, Stafford then proposed an intermediate Victor development known as the Phase 2A. Phase 2A would use interim Conways in a minimally modified wing of

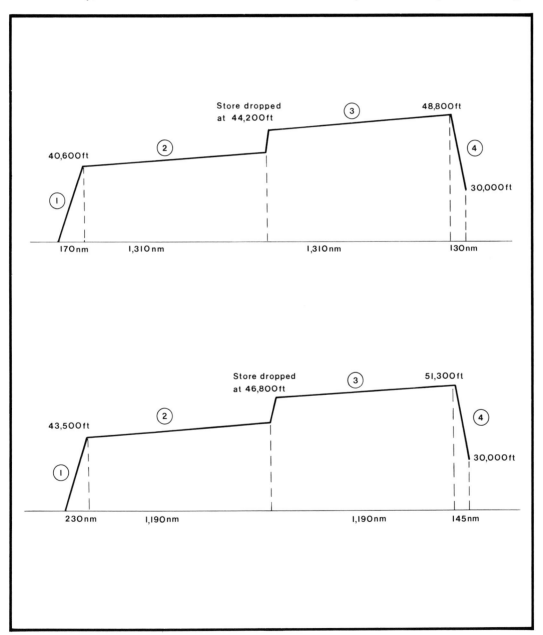

120ft span, with Phase 3 to follow if the improved Conway came up to expectations; if it did not, it could be replaced retrospectively in Phase 2A by Olympus. This compromise so fitted the bill that the Ministry agreed in October to Handley Page supplying the first eight of the second production

batch as basic B1s with Sapphire 7s, followed by the next 25 as Phase 2s with Sapphire 9s. Even more satisfying to the firm was another contract in January 1956 for a further 18 Victors to the as yet undefined Phase 2A standard.

A spanner was then thrown into the works on 9 February when Stafford discovered that the Ministry had decided to cancel all further Sapphire development including Sapphire 9 production. This left Handley Page in a quandary as to what to use in place of Sapphire 9 in Phase 2, but breathing space was bought in March when minor modifications to the Sapphire 7 raised its thrust to 11,000lb. By November the Air Staff had decided to dispense with Phase 2 altogether, and to continue Victor B1 production up to the 25th aircraft (XH667) of the second contract. This gave the company enough time to adapt its production facilities so that the last eight aircraft (XH668-XH 675) could be delivered to the Phase 2A standard as Victor B2s with Conway Co11 engines of 17,250lb static thrust.

It was a good decision to cancel the Sapphire because, for all its qualities, it represented yesterday's technology and the 14,000lb Sapphire 9 would have been the end of the line. The Conway on the other hand promised a whole new generation of powerplants. Redesigned by Rolls-Royce at Barnoldswick from a Napier concept, the Conway was the first large engine to make use of the bypass principle patented by Sir Frank Whittle which combined the best functions of the turbojet and the turboprop. In short, it made the compressor do the work of the airscrew by passing surplus air to that needed for combustion around the outside of the engine to rejoin the hot gases in the jet pipe where it could then cool them down to expand the airflow and thereby the thrust passing out behind. The surplus air also cooled the turbine blades and discs to achieve high thermal efficiency. The result was an engine that offered far greater mass flow at a lower velocity than that produced by a simple turbojet burning fuel at the same rate. To illustrate the point, a production Conway in a Victor B2 weighed about the same as a Sapphire in a B1 yet it produced nearly 60% more thrust for approximately the same fuel consumption.

According to Godfrey Lee, who was made Deputy Chief Designer in 1953, 'the Victor Mk 2 was derived from the Mk 1 by the classic 'stretching process' ie bigger engines, more wing area and higher all-up weight'. To avoid the cost and delay of introducing new centre-section assembly jigs at Radlett, the Victor B2 retained the existing engine bay ribs. Nevertheless, because the Conway was 5in fatter than its predecessor and the air flow going through would increase from 180lb/sec to 280lb/sec, Lee had to fit much deeper intake ducts within. He only just managed it but as the deeper intakes then imposed on a wing spar that had to carry greater aerodynamic loads, Handley Page surrounded each pair of Conways with massive reinforced spectacles forged on a 12,000-ton press from 6ft square slabs of alloy to take the strain. To feed the Sapphires, all the firm had to do was slice off the nose of the wing section and the intake lips fitted entirely within the original profile: to get sufficient airflow into the Conways, the designers had to drop the bottom lip so that the 'chin' now lay below the basic wing contour and had to be faired back into the section further aft. The resulting Victor B2 engine intakes were to be pretty imposing as anyone who has crawled down them will testify.

In May 1957 two development Conways began ground runs in a full-size engine bay behind Victor intakes. Rolls-Royce also carried out its own tests on a quarter-scale model Victor but nevertheless Handley Page was to encounter far greater problems with the Conway behind swept intakes than ever they had with the more basic Sapphire. The Conway was very sensitive to intake velocity distribution and the prototype Victor 2 experienced a great deal of trouble during ground trials when surging produced cannon-like bangs plus flaming jet pipes such that the whole aircraft shook. This was finally cured by work on the engine, 'which was by no means faultless' in Lee's opinion, and by fitting vertical plates in the intakes not far behind the lips to straighten out the swirling air before it entered the compressor. These modifications took two years but the Victor paved the way for civil airliners in getting the Conway installation right.

The Phase 2A wing area had to be increased to 2,600sq ft to maintain an adequate manoeuvre margin above the stall at the higher altitudes attainable with more powerful engines. Cedric Vernon, who succeeded Lee as Chief Aerodynamicist, supervised the increase in Victor B2 wing span from 110ft to 120ft. Instead of just tacking 5ft on to each tip, which would have pushed the swept wing's centre of gravity too far back, Vernon divided the increase into 18in at each wing root and 3ft 6in at each tip to keep the aerodynamic centre in the correct relative position.

Apart from wing and engines, the main changes to the Victor Mk 2 centred around a new constant-frequency ac electrical system. This sounds very mundane but in Godfrey Lee's words, 'an unbelievable improvement followed from going over from dc to ac'. The drawback to the Victor B1's electrical generation system had been that it was frequency wild. The Sapphire-driven alternators could push out a steady voltage but as the engine rpm fluctuated, so the frequency changed which was no use at all. Thus the only service fed directly from the alternators was electrical anti-icing; everything else had to be kept on line via large transformer-rectifiers or inverters which were not only bulky but also had to be cooled.

It fell to the American firm of Sundstrand to answer everyone's prayers when they developed the Constant Speed Drive Unit (CSDU) which, when placed between engines and alternators, kept the frequency constant no matter how much the throttles were altered. Once they appreciated the value of the CSDU, the Air Staff instructed on 8 September 1955 that it be fitted to the Mk 2 V-bombers as quickly as possible. Built under licence by English Electric at Bradford, the CSDU allowed Sam Hall, who was in charge of the Victor 2's electrics, to cure many of the electrical bugbears that had plagued the B1. He was also able to scale down the huge transformer-rectifiers, which were 'a pest'.

The Mk 2 starboard wing stub now housed a Blackburn-Turboméca Artouste auxiliary power unit to act as a self-contained source of power and air for engine starting at far-flung dispersals and to provide airborne emergency power below 25,000ft. It must be said that the Victor's split busbar system was very reliable and even if two alternators failed, the other pair could carry all the essential electrical loads. However, if the engines were blown out and the main alternators came off line either through gross mishandling or from the shock of an exploding nuclear weapon, there was now plenty in reserve. A pair of hydraulic air scoops opened automatically if any two adjacent engines fell below 52% rpm. These retractable intakes, positioned forward of the fin root, drove two Rotax ram-air turbines which provided enough power above 25,000ft to keep essential services such as the powered flying controls functioning while the bomber descended to less rarified levels. Once there, the Air Electronics

Officer (AEO) could start the Artouste to take over essential services until the engines were relit and the main alternators brought back on line. From now on, Mk 2 Victor crews would have the satisfaction of knowing that they could rely on the proverbial belt, braces and piece of string; the improved ac electrical system would also meet the additional needs of electronic countermeasures and the Blue Steel stand-off missile which were then in the offing.

Uprating the Sapphire to 11,000lb had cleared the Victor B1 for take-off up to 195,000lb maximum weight including a bomb bay tank. Higher performance Conway increased this to 204,000lb on the Victor B2 with its pair of bomb bay tanks, or to 223,000lb with underwing drop tanks. The B2 also differed from its predecessor in having roll as well as yaw dampers to counter the added stability problems expected around 60,000ft — the new electrical system improved the efficiency of a variety of services such as the yaw dampers which Godfrey Lee described as 'a pig' on the B1. The Victor B2 flightdeck sported a better autopilot plus a Smiths Military Flight System to rationalise and integrate on two displays all the

Below:
Testing the new enlarged Conway engine intake in the Radlett wind tunnel. Designed in the first place for the Pathfinder Valiant, the Conway was then adapted to power a proposed Vickers transport known as the V1000. When the V1000 was cancelled in 1955, Handley Page was 'encouraged' to build the Victor 2 around the Conway; had the company not done so, the engine might have died on the drawing board and never gone on to power the VC10. *HP Association*

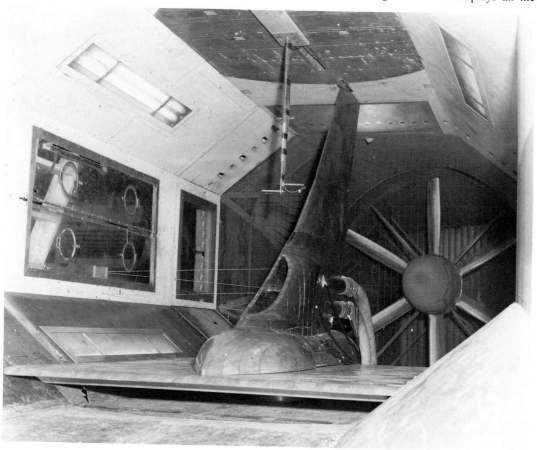

information necessary to control aircraft attitude in all weather conditions and all phases of flight. An improved fuel system also enhanced reliability at height. The end product was a second generation longer-ranging Victor capable of safe operation up to 60,000ft, but its official top speed would be slightly reduced to Mach 0.92 because the aircraft buffeted more once this was reached.

To enhance the B1s, provision was sought for optional installation of take-off rocket boosters at overload weights. The four Sapphires needed a mean ground run of 6,950ft to get a reasonably laden Victor airborne and just over another half-mile to climb it to 50ft, so Rocket-Assisted Take-Off (RATOG) was first proposed by Boscombe in 1955 when it was feared that any appreciable increase in take-off weight would make the margin between unstick and undercarriage/flap limited speeds embarrassingly small. The Victor B1 was only cleared initially for operational use 'in temperate climates' whereas Spec B35/46 had called for a worldwide capability, and RATOG was seen as the most economical means of enabling heavily-laden Victors to operate from hot and high airfields such as Nairobi.

The January 1956 contract for Phase 2A Victors excluded provision for a Victor 2 prototype so XH668 was brought forward on the production line to assume the role. Painted overall in anti-flash white with no roundels and the serial number displayed only on the windbreak inside the entrance door, XH668 made its maiden flight in the hands of Johnny Allam on 20 February 1959. Initial manufacturer's proving trials followed until 3 June when the aircraft was lent to A&AEE for 'preview' handling. XH668 had logged 100hr when it took off around 10.35hrs on 20 August to climb to 52,000ft for a series of high speed turns up to Mach 0.94 over St George's Channel to explore the wing buffet boundary. Up front were two Boscombe test pilots, Sqn Ldrs R. J. Morgan and G. B. Stockman, while down the back were Flt Lts L. N. Williams and R. J. Hannaford plus Handley Page Chief Flight Test Observer Bob Williams checking the Conways. Their progress was monitored intermittently by a ground radar operator at RAF Wartling, and he had just reidentified the Victor at 11.37hrs clocking up around Mach 0.9 when the trace was lost. This was immediately followed by multiple echoes and then XH668 vanished from the sky.

The disappearance of Britain's latest bomber over the Irish Sea conjured up all manner of theories, ranging from the tail falling off again to a highjacking on behalf of an unfriendly agency along the lines of James Bond's *Thunderball*. At a more prosaic level, the search parties had very little to go on because the Victor had maintained radio silence throughout, but the last radar blip tied in with the evidence of the crew of a small coaster who heard what appeared to be two sonic bangs followed by a splash some miles south of their position in St Bride's Bay, Pembrokeshire.

At the request of Farnborough's Accident Investigation Branch, the salvage vessel *Twyford* and four trawlers began searching in that area, yet it took six months of hard winter work in stormy seas before the main wreckage was discovered on the sea bed at a depth of 400ft. Sixteen trawlers using special trawls then scoured the shifting sands, and by 19 November 1960 some 592,610 pieces of Victor had been recovered representing some 70% of the airframe. These pieces were reassembled in a wooden frame at Farnborough; to assist Dr Percy Walker and his analysts, the second Victor prototype (WB775) was dismantled at Park Street and its major components taken down to Farnborough for comparison.

One piece of important evidence was the co-pilot's wristwatch which had stopped immediately on impact at 11.30¾hrs corroborating the radar log; another was the voltmeter which was registering 200V when it was crushed, showing that the main electrical system was not at fault. Two weeks after the accident, XA919 had spontaneously lost both pilots' roof hatches due to a maladjustment of the quick release catches, so for a time it was feared that the same might have happened to XH668 causing the crew to lose consciousness immediately above 50,000ft. But when the wrecked Victor's hatches were eventually retrieved, they were only slightly damaged and appeared to have been intentionally jettisoned below 10,000ft.

It was only after the whole reclaimed jigsaw was put back together again that the true reason for the disaster emerged. When investigators reassembled the wingtips they found that, although the crumpled port pitot head was still in place, the starboard head was missing altogether from its mounting socket. It must therefore have come adrift before the wingtip hit the sea, and vibration tests simulating buffet on a new wingtip confirmed that the retaining collet could have worked loose during repeated high-speed turns allowing the pitot head to fall off. The starboard pitot-static system was particularly important because it fed not only the co-pilot's and navigator's instruments but also the Mach trimmer and stall detector. If the simple hollow tube concerned had suddenly become disconnected around Mach 0.94, a spurious loss of airspeed would have been registered by the Mach trimmer causing it to run from fully out to fully in. At the same time as this depressed the elevators to push the nose down, the stall detector, being no longer inhibited by the protective high speed override switch, would have lowered the nose flaps. In this situation the crew would have stood little chance. At Mach 0.93 around 50,000ft, a Victor B1 sailed along very comfortably like a knife through butter. In similar circumstances, a Victor B2 buffeted and shuddered around most uncomfortably because of its larger wings and bigger intakes. XH668 was probably heaving and rearing around the stops as its crew explored the buffet boundary in steep turns, and the impact of an unexpected massive nose-down movement would have pushed the aircraft quickly beyond the control of its pilots. One of them closed the throttles in a desperate attempt to reduce speed but he must already have been going too fast to pull out of the supersonic dive. So an expensive aircraft and the lives of five men were lost for the want of a twopenny-halfpenny collet; the remedy was to lock the collet positively so that it would not vibrate loose in future under any circumstances. But the fact that the Ministry was willing to spend £2 million on what was probably the greatest salvage operation of its type ever undertaken showed how crucial it was to find out what caused the loss of Britain's foremost deterrent weapon.

To save time, the B2 production line had been established before the B1 orders had been completed: thus the 40th B1, XH619, was rolled out in May 1959 while the second B2, XH669, emerged from Colney Street two weeks before XH668 disappeared. XH669 continued the performance and handling trials so abruptly curtailed over St Bride's Bay, and it had XH670 for company by November. XH671, the 'conference aircraft', was flying by March 1960 prior to

undertaking radio and radar trials, while XH672 acted as a high flying test-bed to sort out remaining snags on the Conway, followed in November 1960 by autopilot development work.

By this time the rocket-assisted take-off concept for B1s had died. De Havilland had produced an 8,000lb variable thrust rocket motor called Spectre to propel the Saunders-Roe SR73 mixed power-plant research interceptor, and by 1957 Victor B1 XA930 was carrying a Spectre pack, complete with tanks for oxidant and fuel, on the ribs between the two Sapphires under each wing. The Spectres were to be jettisoned by parachutes after take-off, and Handley Page tried to install an inflatable cushion underneath, but the recovery trials were not very successful initially; nor did the slightly angled-down rocket motors do anything for the Victor flaps. But all agreed that the aircraft went like a bomb with rocket assistance even after XA930 first flew with large underwing tanks on 27 August 1958. In trials at Hatfield, this fully laden Victor

Below:
The prototype Victor 2, XH668, at Radlett on 13 March 1959. It still retained the B1 fin root but the ram air turbine scoops are extended forward of the fin. XH668 was also distinguished by the big bulges in place of the nose 'nostrils'. During Mk 1 flight trials, the ducting produced a noise described by Hazel as varying between a flute and the roar of an underground train. The bulges on XH668 was an effort to eliminate this but the trouble only disappeared when the pipes were stiffened up and small vortex generators were fitted around the nostril intakes.
Quadrant/Flight

got airborne within 1,600ft and it was almost a soundless speck against the heavy cloud within seconds. Even in warm temperatures, XA930 could get airborne in 3,300ft.

The Spectre programme cost £5.75 million and RATOG had reached the stage of being reflected in Victor flight simulators when the whole project was scrapped. It was certainly not necessary on the Victor B2; handling trials with XH672 had shown that the Conway 17 engine was quite powerful enough and 'even at the higher weights envisaged with Blue Steel and underwing tanks fitted, it should be more than adequate for operations from normal bomber airfields'. Even for the Mk 1s, by October 1960 when the RATOG programme was officially terminated, the valuable operational experience gained by Bomber Command during the Malayan Emergency had proved that a Victor B1 could lift 35,000lb of bombs off a respectable 9,000ft runway such as Tengah. If this could only be achieved by sacrificing range, it was preferable to top up by in-flight refuelling than risk the asymmetric problems of a failure of one Spectre at lift-off. The demise of RATOG also avoided positioning stainless steel fuel tanks and associated rocket paraphernalia around the Commonwealth, though all production Mk 1s had underwing attachment points.

The second B2, XH669, appeared at the 1960 Farnborough Show still minus external serial number but now displaying roundels, fin flashes and, most operationally important of all, an extended tail cone to house Electronic Counter-measures (ECM) equipment. In the period immediately following 1945, Soviet early warning and fighter control radars were such rudimentary affairs operating on single fixed frequencies that Bomber Command Lincolns made do with 'Window' — bundles of tinfoil strips which produced radar echoes equal in magnitude to those of aircraft — to confuse the defences. However, because 80% of all wartime heavy bombers shot down by fighters had received no prior warning of their imminent destruction, and were thereby unable to take evasive action, the Air Staff issued a requirement in June 1947 for a Canberra tail warning radar called Orange Putter. This was followed in May 1948 by an order for a similar piece of kit for the V-force; known as Red Garter, it was designed to give both visual and aural warning of the rearward presence of a contact within 170° in azimuth and 80° in elevation. Space was initially sought to fit Red Garter's aft-facing 18in parabolic scanner in the Victor tail, but it was never installed. Red Garter's scanner was not mechanically strong enough and its scan rate was too low to give satisfactory performance — its range never exceeded 1½ miles nor did it ever achieve a detection rate in excess of 50%. Orange Putter was therefore fitted in its place on aircraft from XA919 onwards to complement the pair of Window dispensers under the front Victor B1 fuselage — the AEO could cut different Window strips in the air to fit the wavelength of whatever radar was threatening. Orange Putter gave frequent false warnings and it was not easy to maintain, but it was better than nothing: 'if we do not go for Orange Putter now', wrote Gp Capt Stuart Menaul, Deputy Director Operations, in June 1954, 'it will be at least 1958 before we have any tail warning device for our V-bombers and operationally this is unacceptable'.

The Victor's H2S radar had a modification called Fishpool which under certain circumstances

Below:
XA930 roars skywards with twin Spectre rocket-pack assistance.

Above:
XH669 was the first production B2, and is seen here with nostrils restored and a new fin root to provide a home for the intakes providing ram air for cooling the rear ECM gear and for anti-icing. This photograph was taken from a Hastings on 8 April 1960.

could detect fighters around and below, so Fishpool together with Orange Putter theoretically met the requirement that warning devices be 'provided to cover at least the whole lower and rear hemisphere'. However the Korean War rudely awoke the RAF to the growth in Soviet air defence potential such that in October 1951 it was belatedly decided to see if it was possible to fit rearward defensive armament on both the Victor and Vulcan after all. Spec B35/46 was therefore amended as follows:

'It is ultimately required to fit tail armament as soon as suitable equipment can be provided. This however will be at some stage in production and is mentioned here for information only. It may be that some simple basic provision could be made in the second prototype to carry the sort of weight involved at the tail end with a view to using this prototype for tail defence development purposes at a later date. Firms are invited to submit any proposals they may have for consideration.'

The rearward gun requirement — Operational Requirement (OR) 1116 — was eventually cancelled on 1 April 1953 but Gp Capt H. P. Broad, Director of Operational Requirements, kept his options open by requesting 'that the planned aerodynamic, structure and power provisions for tail turrets and associated equipment remain in the Victor'. The tail guns had been deleted so as not to delay the introduction of the V-bombers into service, but Gp Capt Broad wanted the provision of tail armament fixtures to remain so that 'we shall be better able to fit new countermeasures equipment to the aircraft at a later date'.

This 'later date' was not far off because Soviet advances in radars and missile-equipped all-weather fighters soon demonstrated that height, speed, Orange Putter and tinfoil strips were no longer sufficient to ensure survival on their own. By 1955 the long term ECM requirement was defined as a centimetric radar jammer (OR 3516), a communications jammer (OR 3520), a metric radar jammer (OR 3521), a tail warning radar (OR 3510), a passive warning radar receiver to determine when Window should be launched (OR 3556), and an automatic Window launcher. Handley Page completed its Victor ECM design study by June 1956 but the equipment itself took so long to develop that it was not until 1958 that the RAF finally decided to amend the Victor B2 Specification to incorporate three large ECM jammers, a passive warning receiver and a tail warning radar. Some bits and pieces could be installed in the H2S scanner bay and rear hatch but jammers the size of dustbins necessitated a new tail cone. With six peripheral aerials, the new cone resembled an old radial engine with a helmet cowling, while right at the back came the tail warning radar scanner radome. Red Garter was finally cancelled in 1956; the Telecommunications Research Establishment at Malvern then took a fighter radar off the shelf around which it built a new V-bomber tail warner known as Red Steer.

The fitment of ECM proved the worth of the new ac electrical system. The new jamming transmitters employed the Carcinatron, a French development in the late 1940s which, by adjusting the voltage to the electrodes, generated noise on a target frequency or spread of frequencies. But jamming demands power, and constant power at that; fortunately, with an output of 32kW from each Victor alternator when the bomber itself normally needed 20kW total, there was enough power in reserve to light the streets of a small town. But large electrical consumers have their

drawbacks — the rear crew instrument panel alone pushed out 3kW of heating. Consequently two Freon units had to be fitted, one in the port wing stub and the other in the old flash-bomb bay, to circulate cooling glycol around the individual jammers and then through heat exchangers fed by ram air — the air intake for rear cooling was positioned in a new fin leading edge extension. Once all the ECM components were fitted, it was estimated that the extra weight would reduce the Victor B2's range by 165 nautical miles.

The sixth B2, XH673, carried out the high weight performance work interspersed by an unscheduled trial on 5 December 1960. On that occasion the irrepressible Allam, with Sqn Ldr R. N. Bates as co-pilot and three test observers down the back, climbed XH673 to 50,000ft for various functioning tests. The bomb doors jammed halfway open so Allam decided to land at RAE Bedford, only to lose radio contact with the airfield. On making contact with Radlett, he decided to return there until he found that the undercarriage would not lower even on the emergency system. Johnny Allam then diverted to Waddington for a belly landing on foam but although the tail-first touchdown was remarkably smooth, the foam strip was too short and a minor

Below:
XL158 at Wittering showing its new ECM-orientated tail with the Red Steer dome right at the back. The aircrew member is wearing a partial pressure jerkin designed to protect him in the event of cockpit pressurisation failure above 50,000ft.

Above:
No 15 Squadron Victors in formation.

fire broke out as the Victor slid to a halt on the dry runway. Both crew and Victor survived and the latter was repaired in time to undertake service trials the following April.

In fact the first 13 Victor B2s were all involved in some development work at the beginning of their lives. XL188 was the first B2 to be delivered to Bomber Command at Cottesmore on 2 November 1961, where a B2 Trials Unit had been formed alongside the B1 squadrons in September. After converting themselves to fly XL188 — and XL165 and XL189 which arrived on 8 November and 16 December respectively — the crews of the Trials Unit under Sqn Ldr John Burleigh carried out 1,000hr of intensive flying trials before Christmas. Thereafter the Unit was renamed 'C' Flight of No 232 OCU in preparation for the arrival of its first B2 students.

'C' Flight had been established at Cottesmore because there was no room for it alongside the rest of No 232 OCU at Gaydon. Its initial graduates went to No 139 'Jamaica' Squadron which re-formed at Wittering on 1 February 1962 with XL231 as its first aircraft. A Victor B2 came off the production line every month and the next unit to receive the B2 was No 100 Squadron which re-formed at Wittering on 1 May 1962. The two squadrons were then joined by 'C' Flight of No 232 OCU which changed its name to the Victor Training Flight on 1 April.

But all these Victor B2 developments had not left the B1 force unscathed. On 1 September 1958, No 15 Squadron had joined No 10 Squadron at Cottesmore where it subsequently acquired nine aircraft from the 1955 contract. A third unit, No 57 Squadron, was re-formed at Honington in Suffolk on 1 January 1959 — it received its first aircraft (XH614) in March and its tenth bomber was to be the last B1, XH667.

Right:
The Red Steer tail warning radar, illustrating the size of the ECM components that Handley Page had to fit into the Victor 2. *Paul Jackson*

Back in October 1958, Bomber Command had urged that ECM be incorporated into the B1s during a retrofit programme whereby up to 12 aircraft at a time would be flown into Radlett, modified, and returned to the front line again. XH587 was allocated to test the necessary modifications, but then the Air Staff decided that the Mk 2 ECM fit need only be retrofitted in the 25 aircraft of the 1955 order. A proposal to convert all the Victor B1s to the full B2 standard was rejected because it would cost well over half the price of a new B2 which, as a result of inflation and development, was estimated at £2.5 million in 1962.

Modified aircraft were to be known as Victor B1As but when XH617 was written off after damage on 19 July 1960, only 24 airframes were in fact converted. Once the last new B1 had been completed on 31 March 1960, XH613 was flown into Radlett from No 15 Squadron to be re-equipped. It completed flight tests in May and was prepared for the final ECM conference on 28 June; by early August the second B1A, XH618, was also ready to return to Cottesmore. Henceforward, B1s and B1As operated side-by-side on No 15 Squadron, as well as at Honington where No 55 Squadron joined No 57 Squadron on 1 September 1960; however, No 10 Squadron remained an almost wholly B1 unit throughout its life.

The B1A was similar to the B1 except that the former had a modified cockpit layout and an enhanced ECM capability. The B1A had a slightly less ambitious ECM fit than the B2, consisting of a passive radar warning receiver, transmitters under the nose floor, jammers in the rear hatch plus a Red Steer tail warning radar in a more rounded but slightly shortened tail. As on the B2s, the B1A's flash-bomb bay housed a Freon glycol cooling system, the condensor of which was cooled by ram air from a ventral intake. It was the blockage of this intake by Window from the front fuselage dispenser that led to the rear ECM cooling duct on the B2 being positioned at the base of the fin.

The B1A ECM equipment was powered from either No 2 or No 3 alternators but they were still frequency wild. The pilot therefore had to maintain around 93% power on the appropriate engine to keep the ECM functioning, and there was a little doll's-eye indicator on the right-hand side of the B1A combing panel which signified when the frequency band was correct. There could be no throttling back of all four engines to out-turn a fighter on the B1A without losing the ECM.

Both Victor B1A and B2 production was completed by April 1963 by which time two Victor prototypes, 50 B1s (of which 24 were converted to B1As) and 34 B2s had come into existence. They

were all first-rate aircraft, which was just as well considering that a Victor B2 in 1961 cost more than 10 Halifaxes in 1945. On the other hand, the nuclear weapons nestling inside each of these Victor bomb bays was 500,000 times more powerful than the conventional bomb of World War 2. Consequently, Minister of Supply Maudling had just grounds for his statement that 'when the Victor gets into the hands of the RAF, it will be the equal in hitting power of any bomber in the world'.

6
Standing Off — Blue Steel and Skybolt

The primary warhead of the Victor B1 was Blue Danube, the first in a family of equally colourfully-named and wholly British-made weapons that became more compact and more powerful over the years. WB775 had completed bombing trials with a simulated Blue Danube in April 1956 but whether the Victor carried atomic or thermonuclear bombs, these lethal devices were all 'free-fall' weapons which meant that their Victor carriers had to approach to within a few miles of the target they were meant to attack. Unfortunately, as surface-to-air missiles proliferated around Soviet targets of value in the decade after 1955, manual deposition of bombs promised to become a less and less attractive option. 'We've got to get away from this free-falling bomb business as quickly as possible', wrote C-in-C Bomber Command in 1952, and a Handley Page proposal for a faster and higher flying Phase 4 Victor was turned down by the Air Staff early in 1957 because, although the bomber promised to be capable of transonic flight, it was unable to carry a stand-off missile.

In March 1956 Avro's Weapons Research Division at Woodford was awarded a development contract for the Blue Steel stand-off bomb to be mounted with the Vulcan and Victor B2. The missile's aerodynamics were sorted out after 23 model test firings, and the first full-scale variant was dropped from a Valiant in 1958 to prove the configuration. The final version of Blue Steel was working by 1960. After being shown at the 1961 Farnborough Display with Blue Steel underneath, XH161 went from Radlett to Woodford to begin compatibility trials with the missile in December 1961. Three Victor B2s — XH674, XH675 and XL161 — were allocated to Blue Steel development trials at Woodford and Edinburgh Field, Adelaide, some 250 miles south of the Woomera range. A&AEE had already given official clearance for carriage of Blue Steel on the Victor, including release of the missile up to Mach 0.84 and 55,000ft; this then allowed XL161 to carry out live firings over Australia.

Having completed B2 production and B1A retrofits by early 1963, Handley Page was then free to modify Victor B2s to carry the stand-off missile. 'The Victor was an awful aeroplane to get Blue Steel on because of its limited ground clearance', said one Avro Weapons Division man, but Handley Page solved the problem if only to thwart Avro which some believed had deliberately set out to build a missile that would be too large to fit under anything except the Vulcan. In the end, Blue Steel ground clearance under an already low-slung Victor was a mere 14in: its carriage demanded no special take-off rotation or landing flare-out technique, just extra care.

Aircraft modified to carry Blue Steel had their existing bomb doors removed and replaced by fairings secured to the fuselage by quick release fasteners: these fairings fitted snugly around the missile with a rubber seal strip in between. Cutaway secondary bomb doors were then fitted which closed after the missile had been fired — thereafter the underside reverted to the normal contours of a conventional Victor bomber.

Inside the bomb bay was the Blue Steel carrier which consisted of a waisted box structure secured by strong points to the roof. The missile was held in place by four crutches mounted at the corners of the carrier; each crutch had a contoured face which was maintained in the correct position relative to the missile by a guide rod. All the main services to the missile (hot air, coolant and arming electrics) passed through the carrier beam. The hydraulic jack attached to the hoist beam in the bomb bay roof was secured to the Pneumatic Release Unit which sent the missile on its way. Blue Steel control panels were fitted inside the cockpit, mainly at the rear crew position, but the flight safety lock switches were mounted alongside the captain.

Right:
The ultimate in end-products: a H-bomb explosion during the 1957/58 Christmas Island tests of Britain's first megaton device.

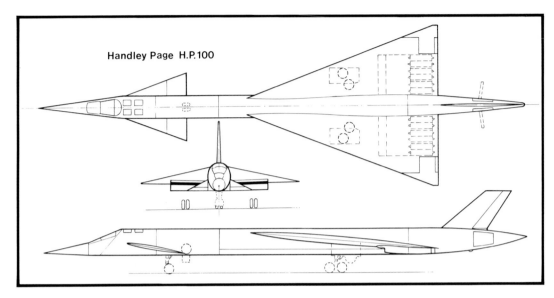

Handley Page H.P.100

Below:
A Blue Steel leaves its servicing and storage bay for transportation out to a Victor. The transporter vehicle carried the missile in lifeboat fashion and when it reached the Victor, the missile was swung outboard on its davits and transferred to an hydraulic loading trolley. The servicing personnel are wearing protective clothing because the Stentor engine was fuelled by High Test Peroxide (HTP) and kerosene, and the former was lethal stuff. Unless handled with surgical care, HTP 'decomposed' of its own accord. Decomposition was a violent eruption as the peroxide gave off oxygen to enable the kerosene to burn at rarified levels, and if HTP leaked on to a man, he could burst into flames.

Above:
The shape of things that never came — the HP100. This was Handley Page's submission for Specification RB156 dated October 1955 which called for a supersonic V-bomber replacement capable of cruising at Mach 2.5, able to climb to 60,000ft after 1,000 miles and having a range of 5,000 miles. Designed by Godfrey Lee, the HP100 was to have been powered by 12 small-diameter turbojets and built of titanium. However, it was rejected in favour of the Avro 730 which was itself cancelled by Duncan Sandys in 1957.

Above right:
A snug fit. Notice that the bottom Blue Steel fin is folded to clear the ground.

The performance penalty with Blue Steel slung underneath was officially given as 2%, yet it is interesting to note that the 1961 Boscombe trials to clear satisfactory release of Blue Steel from a Victor B2 had to be conducted at 51,000ft because the chase plane — one of the latest Javelin all-weather fighters — could not climb any higher. Initially, a Blue Steel Victor could be converted back to the free-fall role within 30hr, but as more and more missile modifications and avionics changes were incorporated, this dualism became less and less realistic over the years.

However, the B2 retrofit programme did more than just fit Blue Steel. Early Victor B2s had been powered by Conway Co 11 engines rated at

Below:

Inching Blue Steel under XL158. Because of the limited ground clearance under a Victor, the top fin of the missile is missing and was only fitted once Blue Steel was mounted to the aircraft. The missile was elevated by hand-pumped hydraulics to meet the carrier beam in the bomb bay, and connecting missile to aircraft took five men about 30min. The little underwing scoop directly above the missile is the air duct for the Artouste auxiliary power plant.

17,250lb thrust but it was feared that they would prove to be insufficient to haul a Blue Steel laden aircraft up to 60,000ft. The addition of Blue Steel did nothing for ceiling, so in 1961 XL159 was delivered to Park Street for installation of uprated Co17s capable of 20,600lb thrust each. Once again the surging problem occurred even though the bypass ratio of the new engine was reduced to match the Victor's limited rib spacing: it was this structural limitation which prevented the Victor from ever realising the full potential of the Co22 which was to be pod-mounted on the VC10. The surging trouble was eventually tracked down, with help from the Farnborough wind tunnel, to vortex shedding from the intake wall; it was cured by removing the walls between the first and second spars together with a spill slot in the lower intake lip.

On completion of Co17 acceptance trials at the end of 1961, XL159 began flying with fixed droop leading edges in February 1962. Like many features on the Victor B1, the automatic nose flaps had been an over-complicated solution to an over-exaggerated problem. Although Doc Lachmann hurried out to California in 1955 to see how

Below:
Over the Black Sheds at Farnborough — a B2 still with nose flaps.

Grumman had managed to fit slats to its thin-winged Skyhawk, Handley Page soon realised that fixed droop leading edges were acceptable at high Mach numbers. The veteran prototype WB775 was flying with fixed droop leading edges in 1959, and when XL159 proved that the stall was still satisfactory and that the drag increment was so small that it could not be measured, there was no longer any need for automatic flaps on the B2. The deletion saved mechanism weight and servicing problems, and fixed droop leading edges also became standard on the B1A. XH620 was the first B1A to be so modified when drooped leading edges were installed by No 15 Squadron personnel in March 1962.

The trials did little to enhance the life of XL159. During a flight from Boscombe on 23 March 1962, Handley Page test pilot Paddy Murphy with Flt Lt J. Waterton as co-pilot managed to get XL159 into a stable stall followed by a flat spin. As the crescent wing shielded the high T tail, the elevators were impotent so Murphy told the three Handley Page test observers down the back to bale out at 10,000ft. Only John Tank in the port seat succeeded in overcoming the 'g' forces after four attempts. Murphy and Waterton fired their ejection seats successfully, but navigator M. P. Evans and observer P. Elwood died when the Victor crashed on a house at Stubton near

Above:
B2R XL158 of No 139 Squadron in its new gloss white finish with pale blue and pink markings and pale blue serial numbers.

Newark, killing two women inside. The fixed droop leading edge was in no way responsible and the only way to have tipped the Victor out of the stall would have been to stream the brake parachute.

Swivel seats and assister cushions were subsequently fitted in the back of the Victor cabin from autumn 1963 onwards. Henceforward, in a crisis, the rear crew could turn towards the exit door and be lifted bodily to their feet by 1,200lb/sq in compressed air fed to an inflatable cushion in their seats. This overcame the 'g' forces and pushed individuals towards the door and out to safety, reducing evacuation time by 75%. Once outside, a static line from the seat activated the crew member's barometric parachute-release device and his emergency oxygen supply.

Fixed droop leading edges with vortex-generating 'turbulators' were incorporated during manufacture on the last production B2s (XM714-XM718), but the remainder were modified during the retrofit programme. The opportunity was also taken to modify and extend the ECM fit following trials in April 1962 when XH671 tested the equipment for compatibility with Blue Steel. Finally, nacelle-like fairings were attached to the upper surfaces of the Victor 2 wing. Designated 'Küchemann carrots' or 'Whitcomb bodies' depending on whether you credited their design to Dr Dietrich Küchemann of RAE or Dr Richard Whitcomb of the Langley Laboratory in America, these fairings 'area-ruled' the wing and acted as fences to improve performance by weakening the shock waves around the wing thereby delaying separation of the boundary layer. The combination of Conway 17 engines and Whitcomb bodies conferred better performance at height on the Blue Steel Victor with minimal weight change: having installed the fairings, Handley Page then found that it could provide increased stowage for the Window dispensers which had to be removed from under the centreline because Blue Steel resented tin-foil strips going into its controls and orifices.

XL164 was the trials aircraft for what was known as the Victor B2R (Retrofit) standard. XL511 was the first B2R to be delivered to Wittering in July 1963, followed by XL512 and XL513, enabling No 139 Squadron to become operational with the missile before the end of the year. These aircraft were finished in high-reflectivity gloss white paint with pale blue and pink national markings and pale blue serial numbers. On average it took 15hr to train a Victor crew in the use of Blue Steel.

Below:
A B2R lifts off. Seeing this, it is not easy to appreciate that Blue Steel was in effect a small aeroplane, weighing about the same as a Meteor fighter; and it was, if anything, more complicated.

As it equipped with B2Rs, No 139 Squadron passed its free-fall B2s back to the retrofit line or to No 100 Squadron. This Squadron received its first B2R, XL160, on 16 January 1964 followed by XH675 on 17 February and then XM717. There was an element of musical chairs in the changes as

aircraft moved back and forth between Wittering units and Radlett. The plan was also affected by the unfortunate crash of XM714 just after it took off from Wittering on 20 March 1963. The blazing wreck missed the tiny village of Barnack by 80yd but five of the six men on board died; only the co-pilot, Flt Lt Jackson, managed to eject and survive. XM714 was replaced by the last Victor of all, XM718, on 2 May, but it was to be a short substitution because XM718 made a heavy-landing at Wittering in October and had to be returned to Radlett for repair. In all, 21 Victor B2s were fully converted to B2Rs.

The Blue Steel inertial navigation system was integrated with the navigation equipment of the parent Victor, and the former was so accurate that

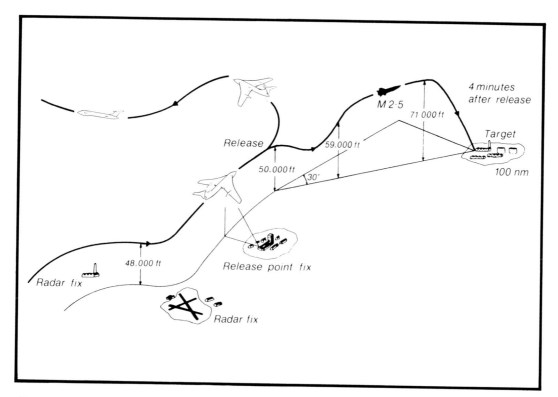

4 minutes
after release

M 2·5
71 000 ft

Target

Release

59.000 ft

50.000 ft

30°

100 nm

48.000 ft

Release point fix

Radar fix

Radar fix

Above:
Blue Steel method of delivery.

the missile navigated the aircraft on the outbound leg while the Nav Radar periodically fed in H2S fixes to realign the system. The inertial navigator suffered from a gyro wander rate of up to 1°/hr, so as near release point as possible the Nav Radar took a final Release Point Fix to update the missile flight rules computer with the exact aircraft position, the direction in which it was heading, airspeed, altitude, acceleration and attitude data, and the relative position of the target. The captain operated a switch to unfold the bottom stabilising fin, and the missile was released from 50,000ft. For 4sec it fell freely for about 300ft to clear the aircraft, and then the Stentor liquid-fuelled rocket motor fired; 2sec later the missile controls unlocked and it accelerated up to its pre-set height.

The Stentor was a relatively inexpensive engine and its main combustion chamber produced 16,000lb of thrust. This was supplemented by a secondary chamber which added an extra 4,000lb thrust, and the pair together were capable of sending the missile up vertically to 110,000ft. However, such a profile was not conducive to range, so the main combustion chamber drove the missile up to 70,000ft where it levelled off; the main chamber then cut out and the secondary took over, this being enough in the rarified air to sustain

a speed of Mach 2.5. In this fashion Blue Steel hurtled along under the control of its flight rules computer, which calculated every change of velocity and direction from ultra-sensitive acceleration measurements made from within the missile. In simple terms the missile knew its distance out and its distance off from the target, and it tried to fly the most direct route in between. Directional control was on the 'twist and steer' principle by which each turn was begun by rolling with the inboard ailerons on the rear mounted delta wing, and then maintained by increasing lift on the small delta-shaped foreplanes. The inertial navigator was forever looking for a particular dive angle to the target, and when it got there after approximately 4min on a 100-mile flight, down the missile went at between Mach 1.5 and Mach 1.8 to penetrate the defences.

Blue Steel was an excellent stand-off weapon in that it required no signals from outside to go about its business, it could not be jammed or diverted by countermeasures, and its profile could be infinitely varied from short distances at very high speed to 200 miles range with a descent speed of Mach 0.8-0.9. On trials in Australia using a distinctive well in the desert as an aiming point, the missile regularly landed within 100yd. It was estimated that a Blue Steel released over London could have put several megatons-worth of H-bomb on to Manchester to within 700yd. 'Out of the last

10 shots at Woomera', said C-in-C Bomber Command in 1963, 'nine have been completely successful. The Blue Steel can stand comparison with any other missile system being developed anywhere in the world.'

By 1959 work was being done on a Blue Steel Mk 2. It had the same forebody as the Mk 1 but propulsion was to be provided by four Bristol Siddeley ramjets at the wingtips plus twin solid fuel booster rockets on top of the main body. This inertially-guided Blue Steel Mk 2 was designed for Mach 3 and a range of 700-800 miles at 70,000ft, but it was taking enough time to get Blue Steel Mk 1 into service on time, not to mention the cost which had risen from an estimated £12.5 million in 1955 to £60 million by September 1960. So the Mk 2 was cancelled in December 1959 after an expenditure of £825,000 — it seemed a wise decision because there was something better in the offing called Skybolt.

The Douglas AGM-87A Skybolt was to be the first air-launched ballistic missile (ALBM). The penetrative qualities of 'air-breathing' missiles such as Blue Steel were much better than those of a manned bomber on its own by virtue of a smaller radar cross-section and much faster speed, but by 1957 an even better option appeared to be the marriage of the bomber and the ballistic missile. Ground-launched ballistic missiles are vulnerable in-so-far as their trajectories are predictable after launch, and there was little scope for hiding their silos in the geographically diminutive British Isles. Skybolt on the other hand offered all the advantages of the ballistic missile in terms of speed, accuracy, relatively small re-entry vehicle and range of up to 1,000 miles while retaining the tactical flexibility of the aircraft. In fact Skybolt could have been launched at many of its wartime targets from over the UK and, unlike the surface-launched ICBM, its carrier could have been recalled at any time before preplanned weapon release point. In the words of Air Minister Julian Amery, 'The V-bombers which we have on order, the Blue Steel which we have on order, and our present plans for Skybolt will carry us well into the seventies'.

In April 1960 the British Minister of Defence announced that he was negotiating the purchase of Skybolt for Bomber Command. At that time the first ALBM was expected to enter USAF service in 1964, and be with the RAF a year later, after a high priority development programme involving $400 million in development costs.

Avro, as associate contractor and manager for Skybolt in Britain, offered two Skybolts under its Vulcan B2 while Handley Page, never to be outdone, tried to fit three under the Victor B2. Radlett soon found this to be impossible because of limited ground clearance beneath the Victor fuselage, but in July 1960 the company put up proposals for the Victor to carry two Skybolts on

Below:
The last production B2 in No 100 Squadron colours at Wittering in summer 1963.

the existing underwing strongpoints. This would have stretched the B2 to its limits, so Handley Page submitted a presentation to the Ministry in January 1962 for follow-on orders for the Victor B. Phase 6 or HP114. These 'Super Victors' had widened centre sections to accommodate larger intakes for more powerful Conway Co22 engines,

improved electrics, large bomb bay fuel tanks and wingtip tanks. The Phase 6 would have carried up to six 'one megaton' Skybolts and been capable of 14hr endurance on standing patrols, for which it

needed a taller and stronger 12-wheel undercarriage designed for take-off weights up to 240,000lb.

At this stage there were 32 Victor B2s on order — the last eight from the B1 programme, 18 from the January 1956 contract plus six added later in consideration of a £9,000 per aircraft price reduction. However, just after officialdom indicated its willingness to allow Handley Page to examine the possibility of fitting Skybolt to the Victor 2 — Peter Wall, Victor Project Engineer in its early days, was sent to act as the firm's representative at Douglas' Santa Monica plant — the Ministry cancelled the additional six on which assembly had already begun at Colney Street. The justification was that back in 1954, the third Review of Plan K had stated that 18 front line V-force squadrons of eight aircraft each would provide a credible deterrent. Each of these 144 aircraft would carry a single free-fall bomb or Blue Steel, so as a Victor with two Skybolts should be able to hit twice as many targets, only 72 aircraft would be needed to constitute a comparable capability.

In 1961 three of these cancelled B2s were quietly reinstated as XL511-XL513, partly because so much work had been done on them that it would have cost nearly as much to recompense Handley Page as to let them enter service, but also because the political climate had changed. After his election victory in 1959, Prime Minister Harold Macmillan asked Duncan Sandys to reorganise the whole British aviation industry because too many individual firms were engaged in wasteful duplication as they chased too few contracts. If British aeronautical companies were to be strong enough to take on their American competitors, they had to pool their resources.

Reorganisation of the airframe side was completed within three months as Bristol came together with Vickers and English Electric to form the British Aircraft Co (BAC), and Hawker Siddeley absorbed de Havilland and Blackburn Aviation. Sandys' stick, apart from his habit of simply locking argumentative groups in rooms until they reached agreement, was the threat to withdraw government aid. His carrot was to promise military contracts such as the TSR2 and support for civil projects such as the VC10 if they combined. In this vein, Sir Frederick Handley Page was given a fourth contract for 27 extra Victor B2s (XM714-XM718, XM745-XM756, XM785-XM794) in the hope that this would induce him to merge with one of the big two aviation combines.

It should have done the trick because the company's net profit for 1961 was a far from exorbitant £190,392, but the old man dug in his heels. He would never have joined Hawker Siddeley easily — 'I don't think any group could have held Frederick Handley Page and Roy Dobson', said Reggie Stafford — and BAC's takeover terms were considered derisory. But there was more in it than personalities and money. Ever his own man, Sir Frederick valued the loyalty of his workforce too highly to leave their fortunes to the mercy of some faceless board of directors over which he held little sway and who might be bent on 'rationalising' Radlett. So he girded his loins for his last great battle of wills against the mandarins of Whitehall, but it would be wrong to cast the latter in a wholly malevolent guise. The potency of nuclear bombers such as the Victor had ensured that the nation would no longer need a large aviation industry to see it through years of war, nor could Britain ever again sustain the luxury of three individual types of V-bomber which had been procured at such a daunting cost. Large sums of public money demanded public accountability and as Sir Frederick found himself unable to bend to the political will, he had to suffer the cancellation of the last 22 of his Victor B2 order. This allowed only XM714-XM718 to be completed.

It is believed that these cancelled aircraft were nominated to go to No 9 and No 12 Squadrons but as only 34 Victor B2s were produced in all, there were only enough aircraft initially free from trials work to equip No 100 and No 139 Squadrons at Wittering plus the Victor Training Flight which moved to Wittering in 1964 as the B1/1A force wound down. There were signs that Sir Frederick was going to be offered a more appropriate sum for 'his' firm, and had he been reassured as to the future of his long-serving employees by reinstatement of the cancelled Victors, he would probably have been won over to a merger with Hawker Siddeley early in 1962. But the opportunity passed with Sir Frederick's death on 21 April 1962. The Victor 2 production line therefore came to a halt when XM718 was delivered to No 100 Squadron on 2 May 1963.

'You have my assurance', Sir Frederick declared on television in 1960, 'that the Victor 2 can carry Skybolt without needing either wing strengthening or undercarriage modification. Already it has flown with the equivalent in weight and drag of two Skybolts under its wings.' He was referring to XA930 with its full drop tanks which approximated to two Skybolts, and this explained the significance of trials to demonstrate XA930's ability to land with only one drop tank in position. Yet despite XA930's efforts and Sir Frederick's brave words, Handley Page never really overcame the problem of mating Skybolt aerodynamically with the Victor. Not that it mattered because at the end of 1962, the Americans cancelled Skybolt and it was decided that Britain would receive Polaris instead.

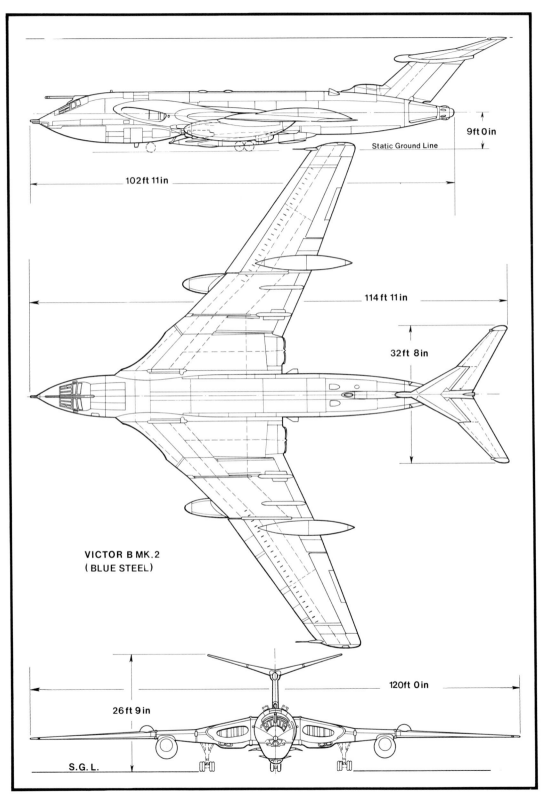

9ft 0in

Static Ground Line

102ft 11in

114 ft 11 in

32ft 8in

VICTOR B MK.2
(BLUE STEEL)

120ft 0in

26ft 9in

S.G.L.

7
Flying the Victor

'From a pilot's point of view', declared chief test pilot Hazelden, 'the Victor wasn't all that much of a problem. In spite of innovations such as powered controls and nose flaps, it flew like any other aeroplane.' Nevertheless, Bomber Command was very particular about who it allowed to operate the shiny crescent bomber. The average age of Victor pilots in 1957 was about 30. First pilots, who were always captains, had to be rated 'above average', be in possession of at least 1,750 first-pilot flying hours, and must have had previous jet as well as four-engined experience, though the latter was considered desirable rather than essential. Co-pilots could get away with 700 first-pilot hours. Among the rear crew, all of whom had to be recommended by their COs and be 'above average', Nav Plotters had to have completed a Canberra tour, Nav Radars to have passed the radar bombing course at Lindholme, and AEOs to have had at least one tour of duty in Bomber, Transport or Coastal Commands. It was an old joke in the early days of the V-force that you needed 2,000 flying hours just to pull the chocks away.

After crew conversion on No 232 OCU, which comprised about six weeks ground school plus a similar period of simulator work and some 40-50 flying hours, a Victor crew was ready to join their squadron. New crews were declared Operational once they had proved their worth, and every six months thereafter their bombing and navigation scores were correlated by Group headquarters. As accuracies improved, a crew would be promoted first to Combat and then to Select status. It was originally intended that Combat and Select crews would serve together for 5¼ and 7½ years respectively, and to provide further incentive the designation Select Star was added for the *crème de la crème*. Select and Select Star designations were eventually changed to Senior and Command, but either way these classifications were awarded only to crews who were consistently good over a period of years.

However, a crew's success factor was dependent to a large extent on the performance of their groundcrews. Each Victor was entrusted to a specific Crew Chief who went with the aircraft whenever it returned to Handley Page and who acted as the sixth member of the crew whenever his bomber landed away from base. Yet in spite of this skilled assistance, all aircrew members were still required to qualify for servicing certificates so that they could inspect, refuel and turn-round their Victor on their own. The hardest part of all was repacking the tail-brake parachute.

To understand what it was like to fly the Victor B1, it is worth following a typical No 15 Squadron B1 training mission in 1960. A Victor crew generally averaged one 5hr training sortie each week, the rest of their time being taken up with ground training, target study or an air test. The crew of five would meet together some 3hr before take-off at the Operations Block, which in the V-force replaced the squadron crewroom as a self-contained centre for briefing, intelligence and flying clothing. The first hour would be spent preparing charts, checking weather and diversion airfields, booking bombing ranges, calculating take-off performance and fuel planning; the Nav Radar would also have spent hours previously building up a full radar prediction for the sortie. The mission this day was to consist of two simulated attacks against radar bomb-score units in Newcastle and East Anglia, followed by two long navigation legs up and down the length of the British Isles. After covering some 2,500 miles, the Victor and its crew would finish up at Cottesmore where they started.

The next hour would be spent devouring a high protein pre-flight meal and kitting out in flying clothing, followed by collection of in-flight rations and embarkation on a small crew coach with its oxygen supply points for pre-oxygenation. Then it was off across the airfield to the waiting Victor that might be on a dispersed pan several miles away. Once there, the Crew Chief would brief on any minor problems or recent rectification work on the aircraft; the captain would sign for his charge on the Form 700 and then walk round the Victor to check some 70 different points externally.

The AEO boarded the bomber first to check that all the systems were safe and then the rest of the crew, complete with bags and rations, would scale the 9ft ladder and strap in. Despite the Boscombe observation in 1958 that Victor 'crew conditions left much to be desired', the Victor flightdeck was in fact the most comfortable of the V-bombers with all crew stations being on the same level. In fact, a *Flight* magazine reporter was sufficiently impressed by the way equipment was very neatly disposed to describe the Victor as 'producing an atmosphere at once spacious and intimate'.

The pilots sat on Martin-Baker Mk 3L ejection seats (cleared for use down to 90kt at runway level) while the rear crew clambered into backward-facing sliding seats confronting their bench of navigational and electronic equipment. Despite several hatch frames at eye level, the forward view from the flightdeck was excellent. The Victor windscreen was a series of long, flat panels which conformed generally to the cabin shape, and Triplex did a fine job in producing laminated Victor windscreens that were not only bulletproof but could also withstand all the strains imposed by high-altitude pressurised flight.

Victor control columns were of the horizontal type and were free both to rotate and slide to operate the powered flying control units via push-pull rods. The main trim control was a three-in-one actuator knob behind the throttles, but each control column also incorporated a high-rate elevator trim switch, a transmit button and an autopilot instinctive cut-out on the inboard handgrip. Depending on the stature of the pilot,

the ejection seat could be raised or lowered and rudder pedals adjusted for leg length. Yet no matter how they sat, neither pilot could see the swept-back wings from the cockpit: it was left to the rear crew to glimpse the outer wings through portholes and to scan the tail through the periscopic sextant in the roof.

Instrument layout was straightforward with a full standard blind-flying panel in front of each pilot and engine gauges in the centre beneath the powered flying control switches on the top of the coaming. The sidewall consoles played host to small throttles for the four engines, inboard of which were levers for the infinitely variable airbrakes. Forward of the port throttles were the undercarriage and flap controls, though these were moved to the centre panel on the Victor B1A and B2. To complete the picture, a half wheel protruded from the bottom right of the first pilot's instrument panel to control nosewheel steering.

Surrounded by all latest strategic bomber gadgetry, the crew would begin the litany of checks; all internal checks from 'pre-flight' to 'shut down' were carried out on a rhythmic challenge

Below:
A Crew Chief on external intercom talks to the crew as they carry out their internal checks. The chap by the left wing is manning the fire extinguisher in case of problems during engine start.

A forward view of the Mk 1 Victor tanker cockpit:

(1) Panel lamps dimmer switch
(2) Zero reader
(3) Emergency hydraulic warning light
(4) Yaw damper control
(5) Bomb bay doors control
(6) Bomb bay doors position indicator
(7) Airbrakes magnetic indicator
(8) Airbrakes position indicator
(9) Flaps position indicator
(10) Accelerometer
(11) Aileron/rudder trim indicator

(12) Elevator position indicator
(13) Port Mk 20B control panel (K2P only)
(14) Pitot head heater switches
(15) Zero reader control unit
(16) Engine fire warning pushbuttons and airframe fire warning lights
(17) PFCU control switches and warning lights
(18) Starboard Mk 20B control panel (K2P only)
(19) Undercarriage position indicator
(20) RATOG control switch ⎫
(21) RATOG master switch ⎬ inoperative
(22) RATOG jettison switch ⎭
(23) Thunderstorm light switch

and response basis, with the AEO reading out each check from his Flight Reference Cards and the appropriate crew member responding with the correct action. The Crew Chief was brought into the chain through the external intercom as he checked, among other things, control surface, bomb door, flap and airbrake serviceability.

Within half an hour, the crew were ready to start engines. With an external ground rig already plugged in, the throttle/HP cock was set to the idling gate, fuel pumps and LP cocks open, the starter master switch at ground, the engine selector switch normally selected to No 3 engine, and the starter button pressed. The crack of igniters would

(24) JPT control switch
(25) Mach trim switch and indicator
(26) RATOG indicators — inoperative
(27) Fuel tank pressure warning light
(28) RATOG warning lights — inoperative
(29) ILS marker light
(30) Outside temperature gauge
(31) Cabin pressure altimeter
(32) Fuel pressure gauge
(33) RPM indicators (four)
(34) JPT gauges (four)
(35) Oil pressure gauges (four)
(36) Windscreen demisting control

(37) Fuel LP warning lights (four)
(38) Flaps emergency control
(39) Undercarriage selector buttons
(40) Flaps control
(41) Thunderstorm light switch
(42) Nosewheel steering control
(43) Nosewheel steering master switch
(44) ILS marker light

be heard over the intercom, the engine would light up at 10% rpm and then accelerate away to idle at 37.5%; each starting cycle took about 30sec. After switching on its alternator, No 3 engine would be opened up to provide 112V dc to start No 2 and 1 engines. Once their alternators were on line, No 3 engine would be thottled back, Nos 1 and 2

engines increased to 75%, and the start cycle repeated for No 4 engine.

When all four engines were turning the external electrics would be disconnected, the remaining systems checked, taxi-clearance obtained from the Tower, and the Crew Chief bade a fond farewell. Then it was off with the parking brake and the throttles opened up to about 50% to get the aircraft underway: once inertia was overcome, idling power was sufficient for taxying. Although the brakes were powerful and smooth and the toe

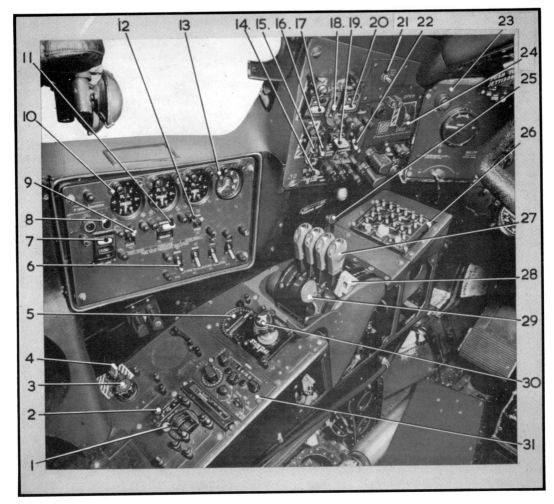

The cockpit, port side:

(1) Windscreen wiper control
(2) Yaw damper control
(3) Panel lamps dimmer
(4) Drop tanks jettison control
(5) Auto-pilot heading selector
(6) Jet pipe temperature control switches (four)
(7) In-flight safety lock switch
(8) In-flight safety lock lights
(9) Port wing fuel vent pressure switch
(10) Fuel vent pressure gauges
(11) Fuselage fuel vent pressure switch
(12) Starboard wing fuel vent pressure switch
(13) Fuel vent temperature gauge
(14) Taxy and landing lamps switch
(15) Emergency decompression switch
(16) ILS switch
(17) Bomb jettison switch
(18) Lower carriers jettison switch
(19) Flashing beacon switch
(20) Abandon aircraft switch
(21) Auto-pilot reset switch
(22) Navigation light switch
(23) First pilot's oxygen regulator
(24) Bomb bay tanks fuel jettison switch and indicator
(25) Throttle friction lever

(26) First pilot's station box
(27) Throttles/HP cocks
(28) Airbrakes control
(29) Throttle gate lever release
(30) Rudder/aileron/elevator trimmer
(31) V/UHF control box

The cockpit, starboard side:

(1) Throttle gate release switch
(2) Airbrakes control
(3) Ditching handle
(4) Throttles/HP cocks
(5) Co-pilot's oxygen regulator
(6) Anti-icing and pressurisation control panel
(7) Aileron/rudder/elevator trimmer
(8) Flowmeter
(9) Flowmeter selector switch
(10) Windscreen spray switch
(11) Probe purge switch
(12) Proportioner and NRV indicators
(13) Mk 4B compass control panel
(14) Co-pilot's station box
(15) Fuel filter switches and warning lights (four)
(16) Windscreen wiper control
(17) Ration heaters switch

pedals nicely situated, only the first pilot could operate the nosewheel steering handle and a strong wrist was required to apply full turning lock.

Pre-take-off checks carried out at the marshalling point — including bone domes on and oxygen masks clamped in place — were just a continuation of the non-stop flow since entering the aircraft and a reminder of how complex bomber operations had become. Among other things nose flaps were selected out, main flaps placed at take-off position and — most important — the power flying controls switched on. Then it was out on to the tyre-scored runway threshold flanked by yellow sodium lights. Count-down started about 30sec before scheduled lift-off time with throttles being opened and the flying pilot checking that the brakes held up to 93%. Then 5, 4, 3, 2, 1 and time to roll. Victor B1

initial acceleration was slow particularly at heavier weights, and the aircraft swung into any crosswind. The aircraft was kept straight initially by nosewheel steering but the rudder became effective at 80kt. Bumping on compressed oleos gave way to a smoother ride as the Victor stretched its wings to fly and the runway lights blurred by. The nosewheel was not raised until rotate speed when slight continuous back pressure brought the bomber effortlessly off the ground at unstick speed around 140kt. With wings kept level the parking brake was applied on the B1 to stop the wheels rotating, the undercarriage and flaps were raised before their limiting speed of 185kt, and the aircraft accelerated away.

Optimum Victor climb speed was 300kt. The Sapphires could be left at take-off power for up to

10min for maximum rate of climb, but to minimise airframe fatigue the Victor was usually climbed at 250kt and 98% rpm up to 10,000ft. Once through the turbulent lower air, speed was increased to 300kt until it was coincident with the high level climb speed of Mach 0.83. On the B1A and B2 a three-position jet pipe temperature control datum could be set to either TAKE-OFF, CLIMB or CRUISE to relieve the pilot of constant throttle adjustment, but there were other checks to make as the Victor powered up through the clouds and into the bright blue skies above. Oxygen flow had to be verified at 10,000ft and cross-checked regularly thereafter along with cabin pressure. Cabin pressure and temperature controls were only within reach of the co-pilot; he was soundly berated if he let the cabin get too hot or too cold.

Nineteen and a half minutes after take-off, 160,000lb Victor B1 would pass through 40,000ft (it took just under half the time at the same weight on a B2). On levelling out, the flying pilot would set cruise-climb rpm and, as fuel was used and the Victor got lighter, it would cruise-climb gently up towards 50,000ft. A subdued background engine hum would be the crew's only accompaniment for the next few hours. Below the high-flying crescent would most likely have been a solid blanket of stratus over the cold North Sea while outside the temperature would have been an inhospitable −47°C. But bright sunshine would have flooded the flightdeck where it was time to check the fuel weight and balance. Sliding out between the pilots (and over the well leading down to the visual bombing position) was a large console containing a

Below:
A Victor takes-off from the old Dambusters base of Scampton in 1961.

formidable array of booster pump switches, fuel group contents gauges and proportioner controls arranged schematically to represent bomb bay, fuselage and port and starboard wing tank groupings. The co-pilot could 'play tunes' on this console because management of a total fuel capacity in excess of the all-up weight of a Halifax was his responsibility. But there was more to it than simply ensuring that the Victor had enough fuel to reach its objective and return with the mandatory reserve of 8,000lb. The co-pilot had to monitor the bomber's three Rotol fuel proportioners, one for each of the fuselage, port and starboard wing groups. These vane-type devices automatically maintained a similar proportion of fuel in each tank such that the aircraft's centre of gravity remained constant. However, to reduce stress on the airframe, bomb bay tank fuel was used in the climb followed by the fuselage group until its contents were down to 3,000lb; after this the wing groups were selected.

The co-pilot, with reference to his slide rule, would also move the fuel around to adjust the Victor's centre of gravity for different stages of flight such as bombing runs or landing. He could cross-feed between the groups or he could burn fuel selectively by bypassing the proportioners and switching individual tank booster pumps on or off. A group of dolls' eyes on the starboard console indicated the position of the proportioners for each tank.

With centre of gravity set for stability on the bombing run, our Victor turns on to its first simulated attack some 35min after leaving the ground. It might be sunny on the flightdeck but whatever the time of day, the rear crew outlook on life could best be described as 'sitting in a coal mine with switches'. The back three were screened

from the pilots by blackout curtains, and the side portholes were usually covered as well to exclude distracting daylight from the world of cathode ray tubes and multifarious dials.

The Victor rear crew sat side-by-side with their backs to the pilots. Looking rearwards, the Nav Radar on the left was mainly responsible for operating the bomber's primary fixing and weapons aiming aid — the Navigation & Bombing System (NBS). The centrepiece of the Victor NBS was the H2S Mk 9A radar developed by EMI. The radar display took the form of a circular map, the scale being changed at the turn of a switch from 1:1 million, 1:½ million or 1:¼ million. At 1:1 million the actual area swept by the transmitted beam covered a circle of 184 miles radius or most of England from Devon to Newcastle, but to see all this the bomber would have needed a 27in diameter screen which was much too large. So a 9in diameter screen was fitted which covered a radial range of 61½ miles, the rest of the available picture being brought into view by means of 'shift'. Shift was applied by a small joystick; if the Nav Radar wanted to view an area of the available picture that was off his screen, he just pulled the joystick towards himself and the whole picture shifted downwards. The display could also be

stabilised so that the ground responses were 'frozen' and the aircraft, represented by the centre of scan rotation, then moved over the radar screen in the direction of track at a rate proportional to the groundspeed.

Information from the H2S was fed into the Navigation & Bombing Computer (NBC) Mk 2 built by AEI. Given the age in which it was built, the NBC was an extremely advanced, miniaturised electro-mechanical device which continuously computed the track, groundspeed, latitude and longitude of the aircraft. Yet although much improved, these avionics were still based on systems used in the Halifax and they were heavy, rugged, analogue and manpower intensive to maintain and operate. The technology was based on triangle solving, the sole purpose being to generate a plan-range for fixing and weapon aiming calculations. Electrically motored pulleys connected metal tape in the shape of a triangle. The hypotenuse was an analogue of the radar range, obtained from the H2S; the adjacent side was an analogue of barometric height leaving a measure of the opposite side to provide the requisite plan-range. The whole was contained in a heavy metal container similar in size and shape to a dustbin, but the 400yd system accuracy was quite sufficient for high-level nuclear strike operations.

As such the NBS was the primary fixing aid because, like the eye, the H2S could actually see where it was over the ground. The NBS could also steer the aircraft and release the bomb load automatically. One of the advantages of the H2S

Below:
A H2S picture of Consett, Co Durham. The aircraft's position is in the centre of the two range circles.

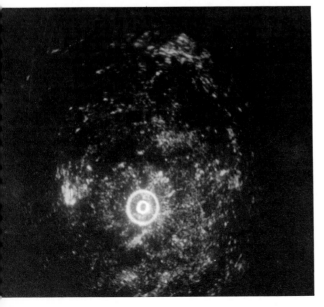

Mk 9A over its wartime predecessors lay in its electronic markers. On the ¼ million bombing scale these markers consisted of a variable range circle and bearing marker whose intersection always defined the electronic centre of the radar screen, and they acted as a very accurate bomb-sight graticule.

Simulated bombing runs could be carried out anywhere, but to have some objective means of assessing accuracy crews usually operated against Radar Bomb Score Units (RBSUs). Our typical Victor training mission might be confined (if that is the right word to apply to a bomber travelling at around 500mph) to targets in eastern England, but the RBSUs moved around for the sake of variety and the procedures were always the same. First the AEO would call up the RBSU with details of the scheduled attack, in this case a road crossing a stream in hilly country. The Nav Radar could sometimes see his aiming point from 160 miles away but the usual procedure was to home to an easily identifiable Initial Point some 60 miles from weapon release where the navigation and bombing computers could be finally updated accurately. At 40 miles to weapon release, the Nav Radar would change over to his larger bombing scale and place the target under his aiming markers by means of his 'joystick'. If the target response was weak or impossible to identify — some targets may be underground — the bombing run could still be pressed home provided there was an identifiable reference point within four miles of the target. The co-ordinate distances of the target from the reference point could be set on 'offset' dials and the bomber automatically homed to the correct release point.

Engine power would be reduced by ½% instalments to get the speed right and the Nav Plotter would call down the ranges, but there was no wartime bombing patter of 'left, left, steady, right'. Once the target or 'offsets' were in, the computer would do the rest down to feeding steering information directly into the autopilot. Up front, the Pilot's Directional Indicator told the flying pilot to fly left or right to keep on the bombing track computed from the back. At the same time, the 'distance to go' and 'time to go' would appear on dials at the navigation panel. When within 40 miles of the target, the ballistics chain of the NBS would come into operation to bring a white flag into the window of the Pilot's Directional Indicator, to open the bomb doors automatically and to release the weapon when the time was right. The computers calculated the forward throw of the bomb, compared this with the track range to the target, and proclaimed the difference as the distance to go. From 20 miles out, a scale in front of the first pilot counted the miles down to release point, the ballistics computer signalled the bomb doors to open just before release, and at approximately seven miles from the high-level target a release pulse would simulate the bomb going on its way.

As the disembodied voice of the Nav Radar called 'bomb gone', the white flag dropped out of the pilot's sight and he would know it was time to 'rack' his Victor round to avoid overflying the detonation, close the bomb doors, and beat a retreat. This technique held good for both high- and low-level Victor bombing, the only difference being that at low-level the pilots could take over and bomb visually if they felt that the Mk 1 eyeball was more finely tuned than the NBS. Either way the Nav Radar switched on a radio tone signal as he approached release point, and when the tone cut off, the RBSU marked the point where the crew would have released their bomb. The RBSU controllers went into their ballistics tables to work out the forward throw and plot the theoretical point of impact. The bombing score was then passed back to the aircraft as a Delta Hotel (Direct Hit) or error in yards: over a six-month classification period, a Combat crew was expected to achieve bombing accuracies to within 650yd, a Select crew to within 400yd, and a Select Star crew to within 350yd. It was then time to turn towards Blackpool before running in for the next bombing run.

Once the crew had had their fill of radar bombing, our Plotter would refine his skills on the initial navigation stage to a point over the Atlantic beyond the Isle of Lewis at 44,000ft. The first Victors carried Gee, which measured the difference in time required for transmissions from ground stations to reach the bomber in flight. This information was displayed on a cathode ray tube and from a special Gee grid overprinted on his map, the navigator would then plot his position to within half a mile. But beacon-orientated aids such as Gee could not only be jammed but they were also of too limited range to be of much accurate use on long-range flights to the USSR. Consequently, Victor Plotters were given self-contained navigational devices known as Green Satin and the Ground Position Indicator (GPI).

Green Satin was a radar navigation aid designed for use between 250ft and 60,000ft, utilising the Doppler principle to provide continuous indication of the Victor's true groundspeed and drift. Simply stated, when electro-magnetic waves are transmitted from an aircraft towards the ground, some of the waves will be reflected back to be received by the aircraft at a different frequency from that at which they were transmitted. The amount of frequency change is proportional to relative motion between the aircraft and the point of reflection on the ground, and if this point of reflection is on the aircraft's track, then the amount of frequency change can be expressed in terms of groundspeed. This was the basis of the Green Satin system which transmitted two beams of short burst pulses simultaneously, one looking forward and one aft of the aircraft, and which could then be measured on return and converted to groundspeed and distance flown. At the same time the aerials were kept in constant alignment with the aircraft's track so that automatic measurement of the angle between the fore and aft axis of the bomber and the fore and aft axis of the aerials provided drift information. Data from Green Satin was fed into the GPI, an electro-mechanical computer which was one of the most intricate and wonderful pieces of kit on the Victor as well as one of the most expensive, which continuously displayed the aircraft's ground position in latitude and longitude on counters.

Taking inherent errors into account, the basic accuracy of the Green Satin/GPI combination was two miles along track and 8-12 miles across track, in every 1,000 miles. To refine this still further the H2S, with its ability to discriminate to within 150ft, was used to update the GPI/NBC regularly. Yet to cater for the day when some or all of these wonderful aids failed, the crew would practice 'secondary' navigation techniques whereby the Green Satin and GPI were monitored by fixes from the radio compass rather than from the radar. As a further back-stop, the Plotter could always turn his eyes to the heavens, if not for inspiration then at least to 'shoot' the stars by astro-navigation. A periscopic sextant could be fitted into the Victor roof and 'astro' was particularly valuable because it relied only upon the unjammable heavens. At night when practising 'limited' navigational techniques, the Nav Radar would shoot the stars to enable the Plotter to calculate fixes to monitor the GPI/NBC. It was somewhat crude but a good crew flying precisely and navigating accurately over a featureless sea could coast in after a long 'limited' navex to within an accuracy of 12 miles.

After two long navigation legs, and having eaten their way through sustaining sandwiches, fruit, chocolate and tins of soup — there were several soup heaters in the Victor which warmed up a tin in 30min very nicely so long as you remembered to punch holes in the top first — the bomber would be at top of descent some 4hr after take-off. Having adjusted the centre of gravity for recovery and selected hot air into the wing leading edges to prevent icing, it was time to close the throttles, pull out the airbrakes and descend. Airbrake setting could be varied to maintain any desired descent slope, but normally the flying pilot brought the Victor down at Mach 0.84/240kt to give a descent rate of 4,000ft/min. A more impressive ear-popping exercise was to descend at Mach 0.9/300kt. This maximum rate of descent angle was so

Above:
A Victor B2 turns towards the setting sun at the start of a night navigation exercise.

steep that care had to be taken to avoid exceeding the top speed limitation: during flight trials, a Victor 2 weighing 160,000lb showed it could descend from 53,400ft to 40,000ft in 2min.

The Victor would run towards Cottesmore at 2,500ft in preparation for a few instrument approaches and overshoots, the pilots flying turn and turn about. On descending through the stratus to level at pattern height, airbrakes would be retracted as speed decayed to 220kt; once in, nose flaps would be manually selected out, the undercarriage would be lowered and 70% set on the engines to give a controlled speed reduction. Below 200kt, the Fowler-type flaps would be set to Take-Off and rpm adjusted to bring the bomber in at a pattern speed around 160kt — as the flaps first travelled rearward and then rotated downwards, there was a delay of about 13sec before any trim changes were felt. Pattern speed was 20kt higher than the threshold speed for the weight; airbrakes and/or power were used to fly the correct approach path, the infinitely variable airbrakes being a wonderful means of controlling speed exactly.

In case the day ever came when they lost adjacent engines, pilots would throttle back two on the same side and fly an asymmetric approach on the other pair. The Victor B1 buffeted severely due to chocking of the appropriate air intakes if two engines were stopped at high level above Mach 0.75, but in the circuit asymmetric flight posed few problems and rudder loads could be held comfortably throughout — power settings on the live side just had to be 10% higher than for a normal approach. The more potent Victor 2 could overshoot on two with take-off flaps and undercarriage down, but this extra power had to be treated with respect. If, following an asymmetric roller landing, all four engines were fully opened too rapidly, the warm pair would respond more quickly than those which had been at flight idle causing a sharp roll and yaw towards the dead engines. It was in such circumstances that XL230 rolled over at Wyton on 10 May 1973, killing the entire crew.

Provided a good approach was made, landing the Victor presented no difficulties even in a 25kt crosswind. On crossing the threshold at around 130kt, the flying pilot would aim to round out, select full airbrakes, call for 'slow cut' on the throttles and place the main wheels on the runway. A prolonged hold-off was not recommended and when the main wheels were firmly down, the nosewheel would be lowered on to the runway with the co-pilot maintaining a moderate push force on the control column to assist nosewheel steering effectiveness. The Victor could be brought to a halt perfectly satisfactorily on the wheel brakes but in emergencies or to reduce the landing run, the 46ft-diameter brake parachute was used. When the nosewheel was firmly on the ground, the brake parachute selector was set to STREAM. Full deployment in the form of a powerful snatch occurred 4-5sec later and retardation was marked down to 70kt. The chute was

Below:
A Victor being marshalled back into its No 15 Squadron dispersal.

jettisoned before leaving the runway by selecting SAFE and if that did not work, setting 50% on the inboard engines would blow it away. Each brake chute was lifed at 25 normal streams.

The crew would then taxi back to their now floodlit dispersal, shut down, and climb out for a welcome leg stretch after 5½hr in their pressurised capsule. They would then be driven away for a debrief, shower and post-flight meal while the Victor, out of its element now, would revert to the loving care of its Crew Chief and groundcrew, and the protective arms of the RAF Police with their guard dogs.

How should the Victor be assessed as a flying machine? First, Boscombe Down was pretty firm about what it should not do:

'Aerobatics, stalling and spinning are prohibited. Speed must not be reduced below that for the onset of pre-stall buffet. At Mach numbers above 0.90, a bank angle of 30° must not be exceeded.'

Below:
A B2 lands and streams at Farnborough. When the parachute was streamed in a strong crosswind, the resulting yaw could be violent and it took quick action on the rudders and nosewheel steering to counteract the swing.

Yet in between these limits the Victor was as pleasant to fly as it was potent. Flying controls were well harmonised, smooth and light as well as very effective throughout the speed range. The elevator trim had a slightly delayed action, but trim changes were small and the airbrakes permitted delicate speed refinements. Flight at high indicated airspeeds presented no special difficulties provided elevator movements were smooth and deliberate, and the initial pre-stall buffet was so unmistakable that lowering the nose and opening the throttles ensured immediate recovery.

Gentle engine handling was particularly advisable at very high altitude or you risked being left with a crescent-shaped glider, but the Victor was very forgiving. Even with half the powered flying controls switched off, there was no restriction on the use of rudder or elevator and sufficient aileron control remained to permit adequate roll manoeuvring up to the limiting Mach number. The aircraft's easy approach and landing qualities were also much appreciated by crews returning in bad weather from long and tiring flights.

Nevertheless, it would be a misjustice to equate docility with ponderousness. *Flight* magazine described the Victor's take-off performance at the 1958 Farnborough Show as 'nothing short of brilliant', and the bomber was so powerful that Boscombe feared that 'the limiting speed for undercarriage and flap was rather low in view of the acceleration available'. Yet the limiting speed in question approximated to the cruising speed of the Avro Lincoln.

At the other extreme, the filling and grinding of all sandwich-constructed external surfaces made the Victor an exceptionally smooth aircraft. Whereas the Canberra B2 was constrained to a top speed of Mach 0.82, the Victor B1 only experienced 'slight buffet' when accelerating past Mach 0.93. In the words of one A&AEE man, 'the Victor's high speed performance is quite remarkable. One has the feeling of sliding effortlessly through the speed range, and no noticeable globules of cold sweat were apparent on any member during the many speed runs done at this unit. In this field the Victor must take pride of place amongst its contemporaries'. Proof of the pudding came on 14 October 1958 when XA932, flown by Wg Cdr 'Hank' Iveson and his No 232 OCU crew, broke the UK-Malta record by covering the 1,310 miles from Farnborough to Luqa in 2hr. Their average speed of 655mph beat the previous best, set by a RN Scimitar fighter, by 67mph: the Victor sported a little sign saying 'Running In — Please Pass' had there been anyone capable of catching up to read it.

The Victor was therefore an unequalled success at the heights and speeds for which it was designed, which probably accounted for the Minister of Supply's cryptic comment in 1957 when discussing high level operations that RAF crews had been 'doing more with the aircraft than they should'. Although the Victor was never to be as nimble as the Vulcan at low level, at height it was nearly as light on its feet. The contemporary Javelin all-weather fighter could barely stagger up to Victor levels before stalling out of the sky, and the Hunter could be eluded with ease. Even when the Lightning came on the scene, it needed a pair of them to take on a snappily-turning Victor with confidence.

In sum the Victor never enjoyed the limelight at air displays in the same way as the Vulcan, but it was nonetheless operationally effective for that. The Victor was a pleasure to fly and it behaved impeccably provided it was handled properly. When serious accidents occasionally happened, they usually resulted from someone being lulled into underestimating the power of the beast they were flying. Perhaps the Victor was disadvantaged in not looking as predatory and sinister as the Vulcan, but to have described the Victor as a 'mean machine' would have been to completely misrepresent its character. After walking round a Victor, the dominant impression was one of its very modest size which belied an extraordinary all-round combination of range, load and performance. While the Vulcan's 'punchy' fighter-type stick set the tone for the delta's personality, so in turn the Victor's spectacle control column exuded an air of old-fashioned dependability. The Victor was more of a grand tourer than a drop-head coupe and there were times when you thought that Frederick Handley Page should have finished the cockpit with an oak panelled fascia. At the end of the day the aircraft was the Rolls-Royce of long-range bombers and in so far as gentlemen go to war nowadays, they could have done no better than to fly there in a Victor.

Below:
A Victor 2 comes into land. Notice the 'Whitcomb bodies' protruding from the trailing edges just outboard of the flaps.

8
Bomber Operations

In 1940, Fighter Command's victory during the Battle of Britain gave Bomber Command the breathing space to develop good aircraft, train crews and evolve effective techniques. With the coming of the nuclear age, time was no longer on Bomber Command's side. In the emphatic words of their C-in-C from 1956, ACM Sir Harry Broadhurst, 'we must have ready in peace the instrument we will need in war. Bomber Command must at all times be ready to fulfil its mission at the drop of a hat. That is our task.'

While Vulcans operated in No 1 Group from bases in South Yorkshire and Lincolnshire, Victors joined the Valiants within No 3 Group. Having decided to 'put a jerk into Bomber Command by bringing in a few fighter people like myself', Sir Harry gave No 3 Group to another ex-air defender, AVM Kenneth 'Bing' Cross.

The No 3 Group HQ was at Mildenhall, Suffolk, and its stations were concentrated in the East Midlands and East Anglia. The original intention was to base the Victor B1s at Bassingbourne, Watton and Honington but the delayed arrival of the Victor into RAF service, plus uncertainty about final numbers, threw this plan back into the melting pot. Thus when 'Broady' gave Cottesmore to the top scoring Allied fighter ace in Europe in World War 2, Gp Capt J. E. 'Johnnie' Johnson, it was earmarked to be a Valiant station. 'I went off to learn to fly the Valiant at Gaydon,' recalled Johnson. 'Then having passed out on the Valiant and returned to Cottesmore, somebody rang me up and said "you're going to get Victors instead" so I had to go back to Gaydon and learn to fly a Victor.'

Cottesmore was then one of 10 Class 1 airfields rebuilt to house the V-force. It had a 9,000ft runway, 200ft wide, with sufficient strength to bear aircraft weights up to 200,000lb, adequate width taxiways and hardstandings for 16 aircraft, modern airfield lighting and landing aids, and new operational, technical and domestic accommodation. Each dispersal was equipped with a fire hydrant, full electrical supplies and a telephone, and there were broad, black tracks on every taxiway to provided unmistakable guidance for taxying aircraft.

Above:
Gp Capt Johnnie Johnson, far right, confers with a No 10 Squadron crew at Cottesmore in September 1958. After his long and successful career on fighters during World War 2 and Korea, Johnson the bomber pilot was very much poacher turned gamekeeper.
Quadrant/Flight

Yet as No 10 Squadron, under the command of Wg Cdr Charles Owen, adjusted to this wonderful new infrastructure, it became clear that there was more to honing the Victor force than the provision of bricks and concrete. Ray Phillips, who captained the fourth Victor crew to go through training before joining No 10 Squadron as a flight commander in June 1958, remembers that they were left to learn for themselves how to get the best out of the bomber operationally. In contrast to the massed formations of World War 2, each Victor crew would have its individual target in a nuclear war and was therefore largely responsible for planning its own tactical approach.

One way of building up the spirit of self-reliance and crew co-operation was to send Victors away from base. Initially they landed at British airfields in Germany or did round trips to Malta, but the first truly foreign 'Lone Ranger' was made on 13 October 1958 when Bing Cross flew XA938 from Gaydon to California to witness the annual

Right:
Johnnie Johnson in a B1 overflying Vandenburg Air Force Base, California, shortly before the first RAF firing of a Thor missile (foreground) in April 1959. Sixty Thor intermediate range ballistic missiles were loaned from the US and positioned in eastern England; in the event of war, they would have blazed a trail for the Victors by wreaking havoc on an enemy's defence system.

Above:
V-bomber main base airfields.

Strategic Air Command (SAC) Bombing Competition. XA938 staged out through Labrador and Nebraska, and on returning seven days later the Air Marshal and his crew covered the 2,480 miles from Canada to Marham in 1min over 4hr.

Victor crews competed regularly with SAC thereafter to spur each other on to better things, and this cross-fertilisation of procedures and ideas flourished as Victor crews increasingly visited North America on training missions. The British Isles had limitations when it came to navigational training because its relatively small and distinctive shape and its densely developed interior offered few challenges to an experienced crew. The snow-covered wastes of Canada on the other hand, being devoid of plentiful features to assist the Nav Radar, were a much more realistic testing ground and consequently the old wartime ferry station at Goose Bay, Labrador, was expanded to act as a base for V-bomber detachments. Victors also operated out of Offutt, Nebraska, on long-range navigation and bombing exercises known as 'Western Rangers', and it was in such skies far from home that Victor crews came of age.

Unfortunately enthusiasm and dedication were not sufficient to keep the V-force credible in the long term. The appearance of low-trajectory, nuclear-tipped medium range missiles in Soviet satellite territories from 1958 threatened to wreak havoc within minutes if all the V-bombers were

concentrated on a handful of airfields. The Defence White Paper of that year therefore revealed that measures were being taken to raise the V-force's 'state of readiness, so as to reduce to the minimum the time needed for take-off'; other action was also being taken 'to increase the security of the bomber force'.

This 'other action' was to disperse the force in flights of four aircraft so that all the deterrent eggs were no longer in 10 small baskets. The original plan was to make 57 UK dispersals available to supplement the Class 1 airfields, supported by 10 regional weapons storage sites and seven regional servicing airfields. These would then be given the wherewithal to maintain the V-force at instant readiness for 30 days.

Although Bing Cross said in an unguarded moment that 'we'll use any runway belonging to anyone, provided its a good one', the '57-Varieties' scheme was so expensive that a compromise had to be reached whereby 26 dispersal airfields ranging from Lossiemouth in the north of Scotland to St Mawgan in Cornwall and Aldergrove in Northern Ireland supplemented the 10 main bases. Quartets of Victors began practising dispersals from Cottesmore in 1959. Facilities away from base were pretty rudimentary at first, but eventually concrete aircraft hardstandings known as Operational Readiness Platforms (ORPs) were laid adjacent to most runway thresholds, purpose-built crew caravans resembling railway sleeping cars were positioned close by, and temporary command posts were established with efficient lines of communication.

The last link in the chain was to scramble Victors from the ORP in double-quick time. Individual starting of the Victor B1s' Sapphire engines was too time-consuming, so Sqn Ldr J. C. Dixon designed the 'Simstart' trolley which, with its great array of batteries, enabled a Crew Chief to start all four engines in rapid succession while his aircrew were strapping in. The Victor B2 retrofit programme subsequently incorporated an internal rapid start facility whereby the captain would press one button and fuel/air combustors would fire up all

Right:
A typical Victor Class 1 airfield. Notice the Operational Readiness Platform (ORP) along the left-hand end of the runway, and the individual bomber dispersals scattered around the airfield to minimise the effects of the conventional air raid.

four Conways in 15sec. All the Victors then had to do was roll forward off the ORP and roar into the sky in line astern.

The first Victor 'scramble' within the postulated 4min warning time of a missile attack was carried out at Cottesmore on 1 April 1959 before Prime Minister Harold Macmillan. Like all new procedures it took a bit of getting used to — some crew members were still strapping in as they passed 18,000ft — but regular repeats soon ensured that everyone got the hang of it. As an illustration, four aircraft scrambles during 1963 averaged 1min 54sec from the order being given to the fourth aircraft lifting off; the best time was 1min 9sec and the worst 2min 47sec.

Bing Cross firmly believed that 'what matters is what you could do and how you show it before you do it'. The deterrent equation began with a close intelligence watch being kept on any potential enemy, and had international tension mounted, so would the readiness posture of the Victors. States of readiness in 1961 ranged from 'Blue Alert', or 30min warning, to the cockpit readiness of 'Amber Alert'. Cottesmore, and later Honington, regularly carried out 'Kinsman' pre-planned deployments to their own dispersals, but the whole V-force also dispersed on no-notice exercises known as 'Mayflights'. On a typical 'Mayflight', no more than four serviceable aircraft would remain at main base, the rest having left for one of eight Victor dispersals. Once in position on the ORP, each bomber was 'combat checked' up to engine start and its door locked; there it stayed, armed

Below:
Victors taxy out at Honington in 1961 to deploy away from the main base.

and ready to go. From then on crews and their support personnel would pass the time in the immediate vicinity of their special caravans by chatting, playing cards or sunbathing (so far as full flying kit would allow). Finally, when the loudspeakers blared out that the alert state had changed to 'Amber', crews would sprint to their aircraft and strap in.

Each Victor was connected to reality by an umbilical tele-scramble link to the Bomber Controller who gave the order to 'Scramble'. Sixteen Sapphires would start simultaneously, throttles would be opened and four bombers would take off in quick succession; long before 4min had passed, there would be nothing to show where they had been save some turbulent, darkened air and the pungent smell of burnt aviation fuel.

Every aircraft would have flown towards its allotted target but it would not have gone beyond a certain line unless further coded orders authorised it to proceed. This was the great strength of the manned bomber — unlike a missile, it could be recalled for use another day, thereby providing scope for political brinkmanship.

Early 'Mayflights' usually ended with a 'Matador' exercise to test the air defences of the UK, but if it had come to the worst, the Victors could have ranged at high level as far east as a little beyond Magnitogorsk on the Ural river. Within this compass lay the strategically vital Volga oilfield, the Ukranian iron and steel-making region, and three-quarters of the 72 cities of the USSR that the 1959 census identified as having populations in excess of 200,000. Looking back, Johnnie Johnson thinks that his aircraft would have been very vulnerable if they had gone in during daylight

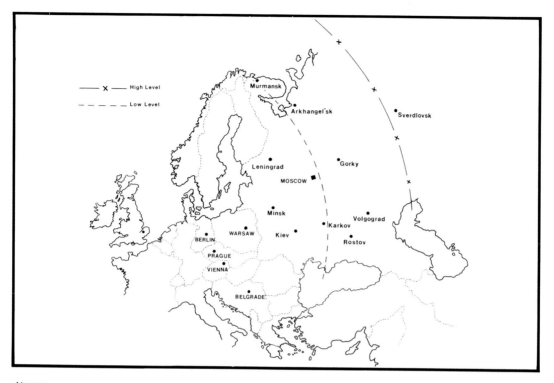

Above:
Maximum Victor coverage at high and low levels, assuming that aircraft recovered to friendly continental or Mediterranean airfields. The Victor was capable of affecting those parts that other bombers could not reach.

independently from the US. But Johnson, whose first-hand experience of bomber and fighter operations was second to none, believes that as many as 85-90% of the V-force would have got through at night as part of a co-ordinated Anglo-US operation. He would have backed his ECM-equipped Victors with their highly skilled and dedicated crews against the Soviet air defences of the time, and Sir Harry Broadhurst was equally convinced that his force was good enough to deter a potential enemy from committing the supreme act of folly. When the Fylingdales Ballistic Missile Early Warning Radar came on line, it became possible to put one Victor and crew from each squadron on permanent Quick Reaction Alert (QRA) at main base ORPs to guard against a surprise attack. At last the Victor force was in a position to live up to Bomber Command's motto of 'strike hard, strike sure' — and on the instant.

But if the Victor had replaced the battleship as the ultimate British deterrent, it also assumed the mantle of the gunboat as well. The Victor's secondary role, as laid down in the Third Revision of OR 229 dated 2 June 1954, was to 'supplement tactical bomber forces if the need arises by

delivering maximum weight of High Explosive bombs by night, and if practicable by day, on targets at relatively short distance from base'. Because the Victor was both highly visible and had the range and speed to stride the globe, it contributed to British prestige in two ways — by impressing friends and by overawing adversaries.

In the cause of friendship, three Victors from No 139 'Jamaica' Squadron would smoke-trail green, yellow and black Jamaican national colours over the Kingston stadium where the Commonwealth Games were held in 1966. But if less convivial surroundings beckoned, the aircraft's conventional bomb load was awesome. The Victor bomb bay was 34ft long, 9ft wide and 7ft deep with the capacity to accommodate 48 1,000lb bombs internally. In the early 1960s, Handley Page designed underwing bomb carriers although they were never manufactured. Each was 45ft long with a 10ft-span tailplane and 20ft-long bomb doors, and they would have increased the Victor's load of 1,000lb bombs to a phenomenal 76. If they had ever been built and fitted, Hazel remembers thinking that the Victor would have been just able to fly from London to Manchester and back. In the end, the RAF restricted the Victor to 35 1,000lb bombs but this was still 14 more than the Vulcan could stow.

Nevertheless it took time to demonstrate even this capability to the world. There were delays in producing the conventional bombing equipment and shortly after the first gear was fitted to XA919 at Boscombe for weapons trials, the aircraft was damaged so the only bombing kit in existence had to be removed and fitted into XA921 instead.

Iron bombs were loaded in groups of four or seven on to septuple carriers before being brought out to the aircraft. There were seven loading points in the bomb bay. Those carriers at loading points 2 and 5 were attached to the bomb bay roof while those at loading points 1, 4 and 6 were suspended some 30in below from special adaptors to stagger release; loading point 3 was reserved for a 10,000lb bomb. Bombs on the carriers could be released individually, in groups, or all together via the '90-Way' Bomb Control Installation which, as its name implied, allowed crews to drop weapons in a variety of combinations and at any timing spacing up to 10sec. Electric pulses initiated the sequencing but no bomb could be released until the one below it had gone.

There is some amusing early flight test film of a simulated 'large store' falling out of a Victor bomb bay, stopping, and jumping back up again before eventually rolling out and away. The Victor's retracting bomb doors were specifically designed so as not to disturb the airflow along the fuselage, but they were so effective that the smooth airflow

Below:
Top: How 35 1,000lb HE bombs were loaded in the Victor bomb bay. The septuple carrier holding bombs 1-7 was fixed at Loading Point 1, bombs 8-15 at Station 2 and so on until right at the back came the carrier with bombs 29-35. Bottom: How a 10,000lb bomb was stowed.

prevented bombs from making a clean exit. Air deflector plates had therefore to be fitted to the front end of the Victor bomb bay. Similar to the gills of a radial engine, they were lowered automatically when the bomb doors were opened, and retracted when the doors were closed, to break up the airflow entering the bomb bay and reduce the pressure build-up which occurred when the doors were opened.

Bombing trials on XA921 were completed in June 1959 when 35 1,000lb bombs were dropped successfully. Henceforward all Victors were cleared for conventional release from 14,000ft upwards, though for extended range the bomb load was reduced to 21,000lb of bombs plus a forward bomb-bay tank at loading point 1.

High-level visual bomb delivery had distinct limitations over cloud-covered Northern Europe but in warmer climates it could be more precise than radar bombing especially against low-radar-response targets such as jungle lairs. The Victor Specification had called for a visual bombing station readily accessible from the navigation station. From his prone position in the aircraft nose, the Nav Plotter had a clear field of view 10° aft of the vertical to the horizontal forward. The Nav Radar would bring the aircraft in towards the target from his H2S and the Plotter would initiate release up to 54,000ft using the T4 visual bombsight into which were fed Green Satin outputs of drift and groundspeed.

Victor crews periodically refined their conventional bombing skills over Libyan ranges on

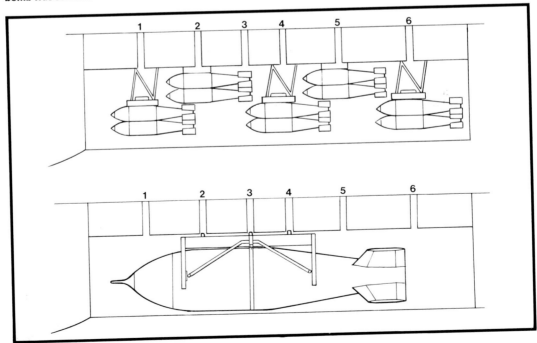

conventional trouble in the Far East while their Vulcan cousins looked after the Middle East. Consequently Victors continued to detach to Butterworth on Exercise 'Profiteer' every year after the Malayan Emergency. Although they did nothing more aggressive than drop bombs on the Song Song and China Rock ranges, they were there not so much to go into action as to be seen to be in a position to do so. 'We were not sure what we were there for because we had no targets', said a No 10 Squadron pilot, but when Victor B1s flew round US bases in the Philippines they were simply demonstrating that Britain had not lost the will or the capability to defend the Commonwealth.

Once Tengah in Singapore was developed as a Class 1 airfield after 1960, the Victors were able to provide strategic nuclear reassurance to Britain's friends who were concerned about the emergence of China as a nuclear power. But iron bombs were of more immediate appeal after 16 September 1963

Left:
Not the RAF's first manned spacecraft but Flt Lt E. G. Howard (a pilot instructor on No 232 OCU) looking down through the optically flat Victor visual bomb-aiming position. The pipe protruding from the tip of the nose supplied pressure during flight to the bellows of the artificial feel system.

Exercise 'Sunspot', but in the true flag-waving tradition Victors were also detached to Butterworth at the end of the Malayan Emergency in the summer of 1960. As Mk 2 aircraft entered service, Cottesmore Victors were assigned to deal with any

Below:
Victor B1A surrounded by its generous 'limited war' load of 35 1,000lb bombs on five carriers. One of the most crucial if rarely appreciated jobs throughout the history of the V-force was that of the RAF Police who guarded the Victors and their weapons around the clock, every day of the year.

when a newly independent Malaysia came under threat from Indonesia. Indonesian 'Badger' bombers began to probe nightly to within five miles of Singapore before turning back, so eight Victors from Cottesmore were sent out in December 1963 to supplement the Far East Air Force. The Victors were positioned to be ready, in official parlance, 'to eliminate Indonesian Air Force capabilities if they launched air attacks against Malaysia or Singapore', and to underline the point XH648, flown by Flt Lt 'Tommy' Thompson and his Cottesmore crew, dropped 35 1,000lb bombs for the benefit of the Far Eastern press. Fortunately, none of the observers appreciated the crew's fear that when the proximity fuse set off the bottom bomb in the stick, it might initiate a chain reaction running back up to the aircraft itself. Suffice to say that their worries were groundless and the crew heard the bombs explode one by one.

Nos 10 and 15 Squadrons disbanded as Victor units. in March and October 1964 respectively following the arrival of all B2s into service, so Honington B1As and their crews found themselves spending more and more time in the Far East. Aircraft tended to remain east and be flown by successive No 55 or No 57 Squadron crews detached for 2½ to three months at a time. When Confrontation reached its climax in autumn 1964, the No 57 Squadron element then on station stayed beyond its allotted span: supported by Vulcan reinforcements, it helped ensure that the war of nerves never escalated out of hand and in so doing demonstrated once again the potency and flexibility of air power.

It was at 17.00hrs on 24 November 1964 that Flt Lt Terry Filing and his No 57 Squadron crew took off from Tengah in XH614. They were scheduled for a 5hr trip with eight 100lb practice

Below:
A Victor B1 of No 10 Squadron flies low over the Malaysian coast in 1960.

bombs, and the initial climb was going well as the aircraft entered a rain cloud at 14,000ft. Suddenly, as the Victor passed 23,000ft, there was a loud bang and a bright flash. The crew's first reaction was that they had been struck by lightning, but then No 1 engine started to run down rapidly and even though there was no fire warning indication, a bright orange glow was reflected from the clouds. Flt Lt Filing immediately initiated the fire drill, closing down Nos 1 and 2 engines as he did so, and turned back towards Singapore.

After some 15sec the orange glow died and it was assumed that the fire had gone out. Then, 15sec later, there was a second bang followed by indications that No 3 engine had failed. Again the fire warning light did not illuminate but this time there was no orange glow.

Below:
B1As of Nos 15 and 57 Squadrons at Tengah during Confrontation. *Roger Brooks*

Above:
B1A XH648 unleashes its 35,000lb bomb load over Song Song Range, Malaysia.

While the co-pilot and AEO concentrated on fuel switching and aligning the electrics to the one remaining engine, Terry Filing had to consider the situation quickly. Two engines appeared to have blown up violently, a third had been flamed out and probably damaged by the explosion, and although the one remaining Sapphire appeared to be serviceable, it did not leave much in reserve. He therefore decided to aim for land and re-light No 2 engine — if that succeeded, then he would try and land the Victor; if not, then the crew would bale out.

At 12,000ft in the descent the Victor broke cloud some 37 miles from base. With 95% set on No 4 engine, height was being lost at 500-800ft/min so it seemed a good time to try and re-light No 2 engine at 10,000ft. On the fourth attempt the engine started.

By now the B1A was at 6,000ft, and with two engines turning, a visual circuit and low speed handling check were carried out. After a final approach at 170kt, the Victor touched down 200ft past the runway threshold at 158kt. The brake chute was streamed and the aircraft finally brought to rest some 20yd off the end of the runway with no further damage. For this 'exceptional feat of

leadership, airmanship and courage', Flt Lt Filing was awarded the AFC.

Post-flight examination revealed that both Nos 1 and 3 engines had disintegrated. Severed fuel lines had caused the fire in No 1 engine but the orange glow had been the only indication because the fire warning system had also been severed by the explosion. Although the Sapphire was generally very reliable in the Far East, XH614 had fallen foul of a tropical phenomenon known as 'centre-line closure'. When flying on full power, the blades of the Sapphire compressor were at maximum stretch with the minimum of blade clearance. If the engine then entered a tropical rainstorm, the injection of super-cooled water caused the compressor casing to cool more rapidly than the rotor. This reduced the clearance of the blade tips still further until they struck the casing with catastrophic results.

The cure for 'centre-line closure' on the Mk 1 Victor was either to increase compressor blade tip clearances or redesign the inside of the engine so that it could accept contact between the casing and the blade tips. As the former would reduce compressor efficiency, the inside of the Sapphire casing was coated with an abrasive ceramic. This not only reduced the rate of heat loss, and thereby the differential between casing and blade cooling rates, but also if contact was made the blade tips would be ground away slightly so that the engine did not disintegrate. It was a good 'fix'.

But if high-level operations were still tenable far from home, they had ceased to be so back in Europe. On 1 May 1960 Gary Powers' U-2 reconnaissance aircraft had been shot down by a Soviet surface-to-air missile (SAM) at a height 'above 68,000ft'. As the Victor B2 could not even climb this far, high-level V-bomber operations would cease to be viable once such missile batteries, together with new all-weather interceptors, mushroomed across the USSR.

The problem in 1963 was that for three years all Bomber Command's plans had been geared to Skybolt. For example, a wizard new comprehensive communications jammer had reached a fairly advanced design stage but it was cancelled because the Treasury deemed it unnecessary for bombers that need never penetrate enemy defences to launch their ALBMs. After the Skybolt hiatus, the RAF considered resurrecting Blue Steel Mk 2 and Handley Page did some Victor compatibility design work on it, but this advanced missile could not be ready in time given that the V-force was only supposed to exist for five or six more years until Polaris entered service.

An improved Red Steer tail warning radar was installed to detect missile approach, and a 'last-ditch' tight turn and jink manoeuvre was evolved to evade impending doom while some cool hand down the back fired Very pistol flares to break an infra-red missile's lock. But the most effective and cheapest method of maintaining credibility was to send the Victors down to low level so that they could penetrate beneath the cover of the new Soviet warning radars, missiles and fighters.

Beginning in March 1963, A&AEE at Boscombe undertook trials with B1A XH618 and a variety of B2s 'to determine the capability of the aircraft for low-level operations and to define appropriate techniques and limitations'. Sustained low-level flying even at high temperatures from Khormaksar, Aden, presented no handling problems, and Boscombe was soon able to recommend clearance for RAF Victor low-level training up to 350kt. 'It was found to be relatively easy to contour follow over the rolling terrain of southwest England by leaving the throttles at a fixed setting and accepting speed variations of 20kt. In clear weather the forward view was adequate but in rain the windscreen wipers were ineffective and the outlook deteriorated markedly. Lack of a terrain avoidance or follow system was an obvious shortcoming.'

A special British H-bomb designed for low-level release was eventually produced for the Vulcan and Buccaneer, but it would arrive too late for the Mk 1 crews at Cottesmore and Honington. They retained their high-level weapons to the end and A&AEE concluded that their best means of delivery was to 'pop-up' just before target release, set a 'constant-attitude climb', and lob the bomb off at a minimum safe height of 9,000ft.

Navigation and bombing equipment in the Victor was not unduly degraded by low-level flight down to 250ft above ground level. In fact the low-level attack phase improved NBS weapon-aiming accuracy to 250yd, and further refinement was possible because pilots could now map read and pass accurate fixes back to the nav team. Crews were initially cleared down to 1,000ft and then to lower levels as they became proficient, with the B1/1A squadrons starting first.

Robert R. Rodwell of *Flight* magazine saw the new style No 57 Squadron training programme from the sixth seat of B1A XH621 while operating out of Tengah in early 1965:

'Fleetingly I saw a junk through the forward windscreen before losing it behind the co-pilot's head. Then our gentle descent from 2,000ft was over, we had turned to starboard and were running in for the coast; there was nothing but the scatter of tiny islands, vast expanses of yellow sand — the tide was out — and a neat green cultivated littoral with wooded hills behind. Aboard XH621 at this low altitude the air-conditioning system was fighting a losing battle with Malaysian heat and the encumbrances with which contemporary military aviators (and their guest) are hung.

'The forward-facing Crew Chief's seat in the Victor is an advance on that in the Vulcan — one has an outside view. The Nav Plotter behind was calling out our safety height — 4,800ft — for this low-level leg. Needless to say, out actual height was only a fraction of this. Although it was made clear before take-off that the speeds and heights at

Below:
The pop-up weapon release manoeuvre for low-level B1A operations.

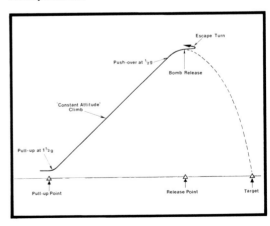

which we were to fly were not necessarily representative of Bomber Command's low-level techniques, I was nevertheless pledged not to mention them. We had flown out from Tengah at 2,000ft and 250kt and had descended substantially for this low-level run, but more specific than that I must not be.

'This brief experience of low-level flight, thrown in during a medium level visual bombing mission over the Song Song range off the coast of northwest Malaysia, was to prove adequately that a large V-bomber can be flown through a contour-hugging pattern at a moderate speed. It left one ready to accept that the contours would be even more closely hugged, and the speed somewhat less moderate, in an operational mission.

'The coastal plain gave way to undulating country. The Nav Plotter, Sqn Ldr W. Milne, No 57 Squadron detachment commander at RAF Tengah, was already calling out instructions. "You're 300yd to the right of track"; later, "Starboard, two miles ahead, a spot height, 730ft, that's the highest ground for about 20 miles." The spot height, a lonely, jutting fang of a tree-clad rock like a small green Gibraltar, disappeared from view behind the captain's head.

'Undulating country was left behind; now we were coming to some grown-up hills. Directly ahead a wooded minor mountain, reaching 2,000ft or so, assumed Himalayan proportions. My sang-froid cracked a bit and sweat ran free, but the Victor gently rose, the green slopes slipped away, and then we were over the top with a few hundred feet to spare and gently going down the other side. "Just missed a birdstrike then", the co-pilot remarked.

'When the 22min low-level run ended, the Victor began its climb to height for the main business of the day. A series of checks were made as the aircraft passed through 10,000ft. After that we levelled off at 26,500ft to keep below a layer of cirrus cloud and skirted the edge of a massive cloud build-up over the Malaysian coast. Flat Aussie accents coming up over the R/T left no doubt about the proprietorship of Butterworth, the base which we were now working, or the range control at Song Song.

'The Nav Plotter squeezed past to crawl into the prone visual bombing position in the nose and for the next 2hr a pair of shoes, heels up, was all that could be seen of him. We had eight 100lb practice bombs to drop from heights a little over 30,000ft. Each time the run was made from 17 to 20 miles out at 295kt indicated air speed and 450kt groundspeed.

'The target, I was told, was a large fluorescent raft. The run-in patter varied only in detail on each successive run; instructions from navigator to pilot interspersed with acknowledgements: "Right — right right — steady — wings level — 3½ miles from release — bombs selected — steady — steady — bomb doors open". There was a slight cobblestone effect as the doors opened and the smooth airflow over the belly was disturbed; the instrument panels began to shimmy on their mountings. Then a "Steady" litany of increasing frequency from the navigator, broken with "Bomb gone". Moments later, by leaning far forward for a craning look back, he could see it fall and called out "Bomb away". The pilot closed the bomb doors and several times the navigator, watching for the burst, was able to give a rough assessment of the bomb's range and bearing from the target before the accurate figures were "sung sung" over the R/T by the range control as a three-character code group. Then it was back to base down the Malacca Straits.'

The Victor B2 was next to be cleared down to low level by Boscombe which found in passing that the 'Küchemann carrots' were beneficial for low-level flight. After a series of low-level Blue Steel firings at Woomera had proved to be '100% effective', the Wittering Wing became operational at low level in 1964. Modifications to individual missiles were not extensive, the main difference from before being that the two combustion chambers now fired together. However, release range was now reduced to 25-30 miles at low level instead of 200 miles high up, and when it was at release point the Victor had to climb sufficiently to give the missile room to fall away before it fired. The Blue Steel then zoomed to 17,000ft, at which point the Stentor cut out, leaving the missile to hurtle down and detonate within a theoretical accuracy of 300yd.

This change in tactics swung the odds back in favour of the Victor force because there was no way that Soviet air defenders could cope with a co-ordinated low-level penetration from anywhere between the North Cape and the Black Sea. To conserve fuel, Victors would have transitted at height to a point just outside the forward extent of Soviet warning radar cover where they would have descended. Once below 1,000ft they would have been shielded by the earth's curvature from radar detection and would have penetrated the vast Soviet coastline unopposed. No Soviet fighter of the time had an airborne radar that could look downwards and pick out a bomber among the ground returns below 5,000ft, so the opposing fighter pilot would have had to rely on eyesight alone. Unfortunately this would have been valueless at night, and even in daylight the amount of low cloud present on an average day in Western Europe would have done little to assist the defences.

This left the radars of the SAM and anti-aircraft batteries as the sole remaining threat. SAM sites had proliferated in the early 1960s to an extent that made high-level bomber operations virtually impossible, but they had been positioned to provide overlapping cover at height only. Consequently there were great gaps in the low-level radar cover between the SAM sites through which the Victors could hope to pass undetected. An AEO could listen out for the searching SAM radars on his warning receiver and, as he could tell in which quadrant they were positioned, the pilot simply altered heading to bypass the threat and the bomber was through the gap, leaving the SAM radar looking fruitlessly for an intruder that never came.

In fact the transition to low level left the Victor AEO with very little to do except to listen out for what was up ahead; to have used the jammers would only have given away the bomber's position. After years of spending millions of roubles perfecting a high-level defence system, the Soviets could mount no bigger threat against a Victor at low level than a soldier on the ground with a rifle. 'In the early days of low level', recalled one Wittering AEO, 'we went in fat, dumb and happy'.

A defender's problem of finding the V-force was compounded still further when the upper surfaces of all Victors were camouflaged in green and grey. XL513, the seventh aircraft to be rectified as a B2R, was the first to be so decked out when it returned from Radlett to No 139 Squadron in December 1963.

The following February the press was invited to Wittering ostensibly to visit No 139 Squadron commanded by Wg Cdr J. G. G. Beddoes. XL513 stood out among its all-white brethren in the words of one observer, 'like a one-armed bandit in a Salvation Army hall', and it made a searing take-off with its Blue Steel snuggled marsupial-fashion. But the presence of the Secretary of State for Air, Hugh Fraser, and Sir John Grandy, C-in-C Bomber Command, turned the occasion from a squadron visit into a detailed briefing on the new low-level V-force.

After describing Bomber Command's alert and readiness posture, AM Grandy said that there were six factors on which the penetration of enemy airspace depended: aircraft performance, evasive routeing, high or low-level capability, electronic countermeasures, the success of earlier strikes in destroying enemy defences, and stand-off weapons. The RAF was capable of them all in 1964 and after a tantalising glimpse of a map of the USSR with a line extending 1,350 miles from Murmansk in the north to Odessa in the south, the C-in-C said that the V-force could penetrate that line anywhere or fly round the ends.

Going low level had, in Mr Fraser's words, given Bomber Command 'an expanded range of

Below:
To minimise detection still further, serials on camouflaged Victors were soon changed to black.

Below:
A typical Victor B2R low-level mission profile.

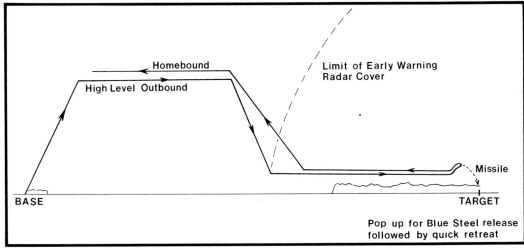

Flt Lt Bob Prothero and his No 100 Squadron crew overfly Wittering.

A No 100 Squadron B2 draws the crowds at an open day. Notice however that the Squadron 'skull and crossbones' crest has disappeared from the fin. In March 1964 Nos 100 and 139 Squadrons' Victors were pooled to form the Wittering Wing, to which was later added the aircraft of the Victor Training Flight after it moved from Cottesmore. Thereafter, aircraft were centrally serviced by Engineering Wing rather than by squadron personnel; if a crew needed a Victor, they were allocated one from the central pool.

options'. With a maximum high-level speed of Mach 0.92, a low-level capability up to 1,500 nautical miles (nm) and a low level dash speed in excess of 400kt, the Victor B2R underlined Sir John's conclusion that, 'penetration by aircraft of Bomber Command of areas covered by the most modern and sophisticated air defence systems could not be successfully prevented'. It all confirmed the Chief of Air Staff's observation on the Victor in 1957 — 'I would say it is probably better for the specific task which it has been built for than anything in the world'.

XL513 at Radlett in its new low-level glossy polyurethane camouflage of dark green and medium sea grey. In all, 3,222 Victor flights took place from Radlett before the airfield closed in 1970.

9
Reconnaissance and Tanking

In addition to the primary nuclear and conventional bombing roles, the Third Revision of the Victor Operational Requirement allocated two more duties to the aircraft:

'Thirdly, earliest production aircraft should be able to be used in the reconnaissance role by day or night having been simply converted to carry cameras, photo-flashes and such electronic reconnaissance equipment as becomes available.

'Fourthly, aircraft should be able to be used in the flight refuelling tanker role having been simply converted to carry extra fuel tanks in lieu of bombs.'

A photo-reconnaissance (PR) conversion kit, capable of installation within one working week and comprising 10 cameras mounted in a pre-loaded trolley, had been a feature of the Victor production specification of 1952. This tentative requirement grew to 15 cameras installed in a bomb bay crate together with the carriage of 150 8in photo-flashes internally plus 110 photo-flashes in external carriers for night PR and survey work. Prototype WB775 undertook PR conversion trials and it appeared at the 1956 Farnborough Show in the cerulean blue colours of the wartime Photographic Reconnaissance Units.

Given the delays in getting the Victor into operational service, it was not surprising that the RAF's strategic reconnaissance (SR) task was given in the first instance to Valiants which were allocated to No 543 Squadron at Wyton in November 1955. Valiants were also to take on the in-flight tanking role but the Victor's reconnaissance potential was not neglected and from March 1958 four Victor B1s plus crews were posted to work alongside No 543 Squadron. Commanded by Wg Cdr Baldwin, these Victors did no visual PR but rather concentrated on radar reconnaissance with three of them carrying a sidescan device known as Yellow Aster. The Victor Radar Reconnaissance Flight survived for a few years but they had so little to do that they were eventually written out of existence.

Nevertheless, Handley Page continued to try and sell the reconnaissance Victor to the RAF and

during summer 1959, XA920 completed Radlett trials with a PR conversion pack culminating in a spectacular half loop into inverted flight to prove the systems under negative gravity. Victor B1 XA918, also acted as test-bed for the Red Neck sideways-looking radar attached to the underwing tank points.

All this effort was rewarded by a conference on the PR role in May 1960 which decided that a Victor be given to Boscombe for reconnaissance trials. XH675 took over PR development from XA920 in October 1961, and it eventually gained approval for the Victor B2 to take off at weights up to 223,000lb with full drop and bomb bay tanks plus cameras. As this extended the range of the reconnaissance Victor 2 by some 40% and the ceiling by 15% over the PR Valiant, it was decided to re-equip No 543 Squadron with Victors. Consequently nine aircraft were modified to a configuration known as the B(SR)2 which consisted of fitting a cylindrical fuel tank at the front and rear of the bomb bay and providing fittings in between to enable any one of four camera crate configurations to be installed for day or night reconnaissance or survey work at heights up to 50,000ft.

These developments were timely because at the end of 1964 the whole Valiant force was grounded when fatigue cracks were found in the wing spars. Vulcan and Victor B2s had no difficulty in assuming the Valiants' bomber duties but the 1965 Statement on Defence did not minimise the 'difficulties in respect of its in-flight refuelling and long-range photographic reconnaissance capabilities'. Fortunately, 'steps are in hand to accelerate the conversion of Victor aircraft for these roles'.

After intensive reworking at Park Street, XL165 made its first flight as a Victor SR2 from Radlett on 23 February 1965. It was inspected at a final conference on 19 March before going on to Boscombe for full operational assessment. At Colney Street, XM718 was repaired after its heavy landing at Wittering the previous October to become the second SR2. XM718 was the only B2R to be converted, albeit partially, to the SR standard, and it too went to Boscombe before joining No 543 Squadron in January 1966.

In the meantime, five other SR2s had arrived at Wyton beginning with XL230 on 18 May 1965, and when XL161 and XL193 were added subsequently — the last on 21 June 1966 — No 543 Squadron was back up to full strength again. Tragically, an open day to celebrate the event eight days later

ended in disaster when XM716, flown by Sqn Ldr 'Dutch' Holland, disintegrated over Warboys as it swept round for a high speed run-in before the press, killing the crew of four.

The Victor SR2 demonstrated its formidable range on 31 May 1966 when the C-in-C Bomber Command, ACM Sir Wallace Kyle, flew back from Piarco, Trinidad, after the Guyanan Independence celebrations; the 3,896 miles to Wyton were covered in 7hr 35min without refuelling.

The crates inside the SR2 bomb bay carried F96 and F49 cameras for day work, and the F89 for night photography. The F96 was specially developed for high altitude use and a fan of eight with

48in lenses provided excellent horizon-to-horizon cover. A quartet of F49s was carried for survey and mapping work. For night reconnaissance, 108 photo-flashes (each of three million candlepower) were carried in three canisters, or 72 flashes in two canisters with a forward bomb bay tank, or 36 flashes in one canister with fore and aft tanks.

The reconnaissance capability of the SR2 was mind-boggling. One Victor could cover the whole UK in 2hr, while four aircraft could survey the whole of the North Atlantic or produce a radar map of an area the size of the USA in 6hr. Airfields could be photographed by radar at night or in fog, with hangars, hardstandings and vehicles being pinpointed in detail. Less wholesome tasks included a survey of Saddleworth Moor during the Moors Murder case, and plotting oil spillage from the *Torrey Canyon*.

The correct speed for normal Victor photography was 240-250kt up to 40,000ft, with the Nav Radar lining up the aircraft and opening the bomb doors while the Plotter made final corrections and called 'Cameras on' from the visual aiming position. One Victor could bring back 10,000ft of exposed film to be handed over to the Wyton Photo Factory for processing, but No 543 Squadron also experimented with infra-red, 'false colour' and rapid processing film. However, there was never any intention that the Squadron would reconnoitre over the Soviet Union; the U-2 incident had seen to that and consequently the SR

Victor carried a very limited ECM fit. Visual photography was confined to 'friendly' skies and to such work as photographing ships in the North Sea or surveying Denmark in 1967.

Once it became clear that such visual work could be carried out just as well and often more cheaply by PR Canberras, camera crates were removed from the Victors in 1970 and radar reconnaissance came into much more prominence. As the Soviet Navy grew in strength, so the RN demanded more and more intelligence on its whereabouts. This was where No 543 Squadron excelled because an SR2 could cover an area of 400,000sq miles in 8hr and a Nav Radar could plot the position of every vessel in the Mediterranean on one sortie from his H2S, thereby enabling Defence Minister Denis Healey to make his famous statement that the British knew the position of every Soviet ship in the Mediterranean and that they could cope with them all if the need arose.

If the Victor was in a good position to become a reconnaissance platform, it was a bit harder

Above:
The business end of the SR2. The camera crate is sandwiched between cylindrical long-range fuel tanks.

pressed to immediately assume the air refuelling role when the Valiants folded. Flight refuelling was introduced into the RAF initially for the benefit of short-range fighters. A Vampire 9 ferrying the 8,618 miles to Singapore in 1953 would have had to stage through 16 airfields in France, Tunis, Tripoli, Libya, Egypt, Iraq, Trucial Oman, Pakistan, India, Burma and Malaya, but as Britain withdrew from colonial possessions and found previously friendly airspace denied to it, the RAF stabilised on an eastward chain of staging posts in Malta, Cyprus, the Persian Gulf and the island of Gan in the Indian Ocean. Thirsty fighters needed airborne refuelling to cover the intervening legs between these bases, and it was then but a short step to refuelling non-stop to do away with all the en route ground servicing parties and associated support.

On 5 January 1954 the Air Staff decided that Victors and Vulcans should be capable of taking on fuel while airborne as well. At first this was seen as a means of enabling V-bombers to reach their Soviet targets by longer but more secure routes,

but in-flight refuelling justification soon swung towards reinforcing Aden within 7hr (with one 'precautionary' flight refuelling), Gan in 11hr (with two refuellings) and Singapore in 15hr (with three) to protect the Commonwealth.

All production Victors left Radlett with a fuel system adapted for flight refuelling, and a partial trial of a refuelling probe was planned to be installed on XA921 at Boscombe in 1958. This programme was delayed when XA921 was suddenly switched to conventional bombing trials, so the necessary modifications were made to XA930 instead. XA930 first flew with probe and underwing tanks on 27 August 1958 and after appearing thus at the Farnborough Show a week later, the aircraft was progressively modified over the next year with three different lengths of nose probe. In November 1960, after eight months of trials with a Valiant tanker, the intermediate probe length was chosen and the Victor cleared to receive fuel at 220-240kt up to 34,000ft, this being the maximum capability of the Valiant tanker at high weights.

The first refuelling probe was fitted to an operational B1A when XH620 was modified by personnel of No 15 Squadron in March 1962. The Victor probe stuck out like a unicorn's horn from

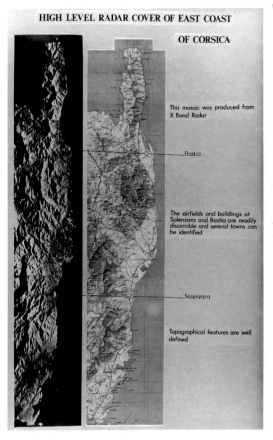

HIGH LEVEL RADAR COVER OF EAST COAST
OF CORSICA

This mosaic was produced from
X Band Radar

Bastia

The airfields and buildings at
Solenzara and Bastia are readily
discernible and several towns can
be identified

Solenzara

Topographical features are well
defined

RECONNAISSANCE
IN THE MARITIME
ROLE

Left:
The detail obtainable from the SR2's radar is illustrated by this comparison between a post-flight radar mosaic (left) and an equivalent conventional map of the Corsican coast.

Right:
XA930 with its trial fit of nose probe and underwing tanks. *HP Association*

Centre right:
XA918 as photographed in 1964 sporting two underwing refuelling pods. The bulge housing the ventral hose-drogue unit is just visible at the rear of the bomb bay. *HP Association*

the top of the fuselage and fuel ran to the tanks at a maximum rate of 480gal/min via a pipe that passed along the cockpit roof over the Nav Radar's head. No 57 Squadron B1As were the next to be modified but Victor B2s came off the production line with probes attached.

In 1962 it was decided to use first-generation Victors as tankers once they withdrew from front line bomber service. Early in 1964 the second production B1, XA918, was fitted with two fuel tanks in the bomb bay, a retractable Flight Refuelling Ltd FR17 hose-drogue pack in the bomb bay, and two FR20B hose-drogue pods beneath the wings. At first it was intended to make these pods interchangeable with underwing tanks on the standard strong points, but this was then found to bring the trailing drogues dangerously near the tail so the FR20B pods were positioned further outboard. For those of a statistical bent, the 13ft 6in-long Mk 20B pod was fitted 13ft 6in from the Victor wingtip, but no drop tanks were carried on Mk 1s apart from trials aircraft XA930 because the Sapphire engines were too under-powered to cope.

XA918 first flew as a tanker on 8 July 1964. Modifications were completed in August 1964 and the plan was to convert B1s and B1As to the XA918 standard as aircraft were released by the disbandment of No 10 and No 15 Squadrons. Unfortunately the sudden demise of the Valiant left a tanker vacuum, and Handley Page worked day and night on an accelerated programme to convert six B1As to two-point tankers with FR20B wing pods only. A fully loaded pod weighed 2,000lb and it included a two-bladed ram air turbine to provide hydraulic and fuel pressure via a

Left:
A typical No 543 Squadron maritime radar reconnaissance (MRR) flight profile around 40,000ft over the Norwegian Sea. The Nav Radar could differentiate between large, medium and small surface vessels and any interesting contacts would be passed to a Shackleton for more detailed scrutiny at low level.

Right:
An SR2 investigates a ship for itself.

Above:
XA918 undertaking ventral refuelling trials with a Vulcan B2.

gear box, a 145gal fuel tank replenished from the aircraft's fuel system, and a hose drum unit around which was wound a 51ft hose with a 1½in internal bore. The end of the hose was connected to the Mk VIII drogue coupling to enable fuel to be passed to a receiver up to a rate of 1,200lb/min. Coloured lights to act as 'traffic indicators' were fitted to each pod so that refuelling could be carried out in radio silence, and the only other addition to the aircraft was a second bomb bay tank to give a total transferable fuel load of 48,000lb.

These six interim tankers were initially designated B(K)1As and Radlett laboured to such effect that the first, XH620, was flying on 28 April 1965. Priority A&AEE handling trials with Lightning and Sea Vixen contacts were concluded by 21 May during which the presence of a Mk 20B pod under each wing was found to make no significant changes to the Victor's flying characteristics. The B(K)1A was pleasant to fly and Boscombe cleared it for a maximum take-off weight of 185,000lb and a top speed of 330kt/Mach 0.93.

B(K)1As were delivered to No 55 Squadron which moved from Honington to Marham on 24 May 1965. No 55 Squadron was still a bomber squadron at the time, and the six interim tankers retained their bombing capability. Crews converted to their new tanking role in time to ferry Lightnings of No 74 Squadron out to Akrotiri, and those of No 19 Squadron back to Leconfield, in August 1965. All six B(K)1As were at Marham by the following month and during their first 1½ years in service, No 55 Squadron took part in 39 overseas exercises and transferred 6,718,700lb of

Above:
Servicing a wing pod drogue at a sunny airfield down the route. To make contact, a receiver pilot simply (or frantically) flew his probe nozzle into the conical drogue while overtaking the Victor by 2-5kt. Inside the drogue was a reception coupling, a spring-loaded cut-off valve and toggle-arm rollers. As the nozzle entered, its domed nose pushed open the spring-loaded cut-off valve. With the valves on each side of the connection open, the toggle-arm rollers engaged the external groove in the nozzle shell, locking all elements in place and aligning them correctly for fuel transfer. The nozzle also contained a 'weak-link' which broke in the event of excessive loads during transfer.

fuel from their 12 drogues during 3,143 wet contacts.

On 2 November 1965 the first three-point Victor tanker conversion, XA937, took to the air. The 10 Victors initially modified to this configuration were selected from the original B1 production batch and were in consequence eventually known as Victor K1s. Although externally similar to the B(K)1A, the K1s were very different internally. They

Above:
A Victor K1 of No 57 Squadron. Particular care had to be taken during taxying and landing in crosswinds because of the limited ground clearance of the wing refuelling pods.

carried Mk 20B wing pods and nose probe, but most significantly they lost their bombing capability when their bomb doors were removed and two 15,300lb fuel tanks plus a Mk 17 Hose Drum Unit (HDU) were fitted in their bomb bays.

The Mk 17 HDU was mounted on a retractable platform so that the scoop containing the hose and drogue could be lowered by a jack connected to the old bomb door hydraulics. The HDU initially carried a 93ft hose with a 3in internal bore but this was soon found to snake violently when disturbed by unstable air, much to the amusement (or horror) of receiver pilots who were then treated to the interesting sight of a hose which fluctuated from the near vertical to the horizontal. After Boscombe trials, the problem was solved by shortening the hose to 80ft and fitting a modified drogue.

No 57 Squadron followed No 55 Squadron over to Marham in December 1965. No 57 Squadron was the first to receive a Victor K1 on 14 February 1966 and subsequent additions enabled No 57 Squadron to become operational as a tanker squadron on 1 June. Their HDUs were generally reserved for large aircraft and in October 1966, No 57 Squadron successfully proved the ventral arrangement in trials with a VC10 shortly after the strategic transport entered service with the original Victor unit, No 10 Squadron.

A Victor K1 could carry enough fuel to keep a Lightning airborne for 17hr and tanker support thereby considerably extended the air defender's range, flexibility and effectiveness. Dotted around the coast of Britain were six 'towlines' to which

fighters would be directed by their air defence radar controllers. The Victor Nav Radar, who monitored the refuelling exercise, could watch thirsty contacts approach by using the Fishpool mode on his H2S radar. As they closed, he could trail the winghoses in 20sec before passing sustaining fuel — the only thing he did not give was Green Shield stamps.

On very long overseas flights, two Victors would fly in company with the fighters, each refuelling a 'chick' about every 30min. As the Victors were themselves depleted, one tanker would top up the other via the HDU before returning to base. The second Victor would continue with the fighters, replenishing as required, until it too was replaced by a new pair of tankers. This process was repeated down the route.

As B1A bombers returned to Radlett, 14 were converted to three-point tankers known eventually as K1As. The first Valiant tanker unit, No 214 Squadron, re-formed at Marham on 1 October 1966 with Victor K1s, and No 55 Squadron exchanged its interim tankers for K1As from January 1967 onwards. At the same time, No 55 Squadron relinquished its tanker conversion responsibilities to the Tanker Training Flight (TTF) which took over three of the two-point tankers while the remaining trio were distributed around the squadrons to act as 'hacks'; these aircraft were known henceforward as B1A (K2P)s. In May 1970, the TTF was redesignated No 232 OCU.

By the time the last tanker conversion was completed in June 1967, Handley Page had produced six two-point and 24 three-point Victor tankers. They were all a considerable improvement over their predecessors because the Valiant did not have wing pods and the three-point Victor could dispense twice as much fuel.

In June 1968 a Hastings and Victor K1 XA927 from No 57 Squadron represented all the aircraft ever built by Handley Page in the Queen's Review static display at Abingdon. Overhead six B2Rs from Wittering led a 24-ship flypast, but it was to be the swansong of the Victor bomber because from now on, the maintenance of the Handley Page tradition lay with the tanker on the ground.

Every day from 1963, two Victor B2Rs — one from each of Nos 100 and 139 Squadrons — had sat on the Wittering ORP with their crews on QRA. Two dozen practice alerts codenamed 'EDOM' might be called in an average month, half of them being up to engine start and nearly one-quarter involving taxying to the take-off position. But whereas the Vulcan continued in service after RN Polaris submarines took over strategic deterrent responsibility, metal fatigue killed off the Victor bomber as surely as it did the Valiant.

In their quest for better performance after 1945, aircraft designers became so weight-conscious that they rejected the old wartime light aluminium alloys in favour of new high strength, light zinc-bearing forged alloys known as DTD 683 and DTD 687. These double heat-treated plates were extremely strong as well as light, but their long-term properties were unknown and it was eventually found that they became brittle with a

Below:
XH615, a B1A(K2P) tanker, in the colours of No 232 OCU. *Steve Millard*

high propensity to stress fatigue. Anodising had no effect but lanoline prolonged fatigue life so it was used in the manufacture of the Victor just as it had coated the 'Yellow Peril'. Yet in fairness to all concerned, when the Victors were built there was not the range of alternatives there is today. 'Because they were high strength alloys', said Ken Pratt, 'they were the only things you could use in

big structure members and skins that enabled you to get the structural weight to something half decent. If we had known then what we know now about DTD 683 (used in forgings and extrusions) we would not have used it, but if we hadn't used 683 the aircraft would have been much heavier or we would have a gap of 7-10 years before alternatives became available to build an aeroplane that did as well as the Victor did.'

Because a bomber did not have as long an operational life as a transport in terms of flying hours, the specialists believed that there were adequate safeguards against stress cracking and premature fatigue failure. 'We had a tremendously redundant structure', said Godfrey Lee, 'with distributed flanges and a multitude of bolts holding the wings together, unlike the Valiant which was dependent on a few spars.' But a complete change in role altered the situation. The Victor was designed to spend the majority of its operational life in the calm upper air, encountering turbulence simply in the climb and descent, but from 1964 the aircraft found themselves in a completely new low-level environment. Handley Page considered proposals to modify their bomber to cope with its new flight regime. One was to reduce span, but it is very difficult to reduce span on a swept-wing

aircraft without generating a host of new problems and anyway a complete rebuild would have been necessary to strengthen the structure.

Unfortunately whereas the massive strength of the Vulcan wing, plus reinforcement in anticipation of Skybolt, would sustain the delta at low level into the 1980s, the Victor had a more flexible wing. The Victor was more comfortable to fly at low level because it rode out the gusts and turbulence as the wings flexed up and down like giant shock absorbers. 'We used to practice one manoeuvre', recalled a No 100 Squadron captain, 'which simulated the failure of the Blue Steel motor. We would rush in at 350kt, pull up at 1.5g to 11,000ft and then release the missile on the Nav Radar's call like a free-fall bomb. This was all very well, but whenever we pulled up from low level, you could hear the wings crack.'

Thus by the time Nos 100 and 139 Squadrons disbanded on 1 October and 31 December 1968 respectively, the lower boom forgings which provided the mainplane attachments were cracked on most B2Rs. All but two aircraft were therefore flown down to Radlett to be mothballed. After 53 years, the sight and sound of a Handley Page bomber was to be no more.

Top right:
A B2R in flight with the Blue Steel bottom fin folded. A low level Terrain-Following Radar (TFR) was trialled on XL164 over the Libyan desert. The radar was housed in a cone on the Victor's nose, and Ken Pratt observed that 'we had an interesting time fitting TFR and making it work'. Unfortunately the terrain avoidance device was never to prove really effective on the B2R force and crews had to continue to contour fly visually until the Wittering Wing disbanded.

Above right:
A B2R lands and streams while a Wessex helicopter crew stands and watches. Notice the fully extended airbrakes which were copied on the Buccaneer.

Centre right:
Wg Cdr Harry Archer AFC, OC No 100 Squadron, kneels at far left, front row, with the Downey and Goodman crews on 22 August 1967 prior to their departure for an air display in Toronto. The winged Lawrence Minot Trophy (foreground) was the premier award in the annual Anglo-American Medium Bomber Force Bombing and Navigation Competition, and it had been won by No 100 Squadron the previous March. Capt Lawrence Minot had been killed on air combat in 1917 while serving with No 57 Squadron, and it was most appropriate that No 57 Squadron should win the Trophy in 1965 and 1966 during its last two years as a medium bomber squadron.

Right:
A good view of the 'warty' tail of the B2R. The technician on the ladder is looking through the 'back hatch', into the rear equipment compartment where all manner of goodies including reserve brake parachute could be stowed on overseas 'rangers'. The strakes on top of the airbrakes were added to improve efficiency.

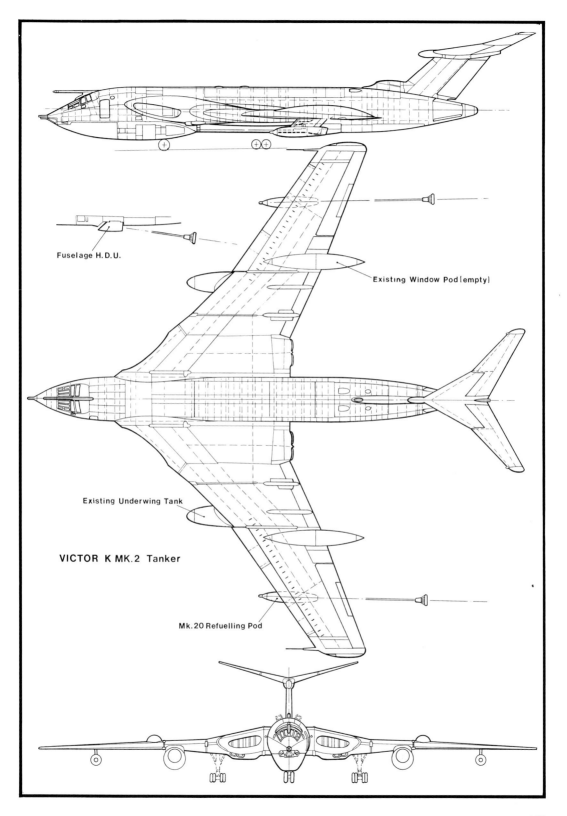

Fuselage H.D.U.

Existing Window Pod (empty)

Existing Underwing Tank

VICTOR K MK.2 Tanker

Mk.20 Refuelling Pod

10
Variations on a Theme

No Victors ever served outside the RAF. In March 1954 the Australian Air Minister outlined long-term plans for the RAAF to operate 24 V-bombers from a ring of airfields in North Australia, and Reggie Stafford paid a visit down-under in 1959 to try and sell the Victor B2. But nothing came of all this because, basically, if a nation did not possess nuclear weapons it did not need the luxury of a Victor. The only foreigners who got 'extremely interested' in the Victor were the South Africans who sent two SAAF officers to fly XH670 on 23 October 1961. In the end though, the South African requirement was met by a Buccaneer order in 1963.

Handley Page set greater store on a transport version of the Victor. Two such variants of the HP80 were proposed as early as 1950 by the relatively simple process of combining a new fuselage with the bomber's wings, engines and tail. The first of these, the HP96 military transport, had a widened and longer fuselage wherein two compartments separated by toilets could accommodate 85 troops, or cargo could be stowed through tail doors.

The second derivative was the HP97 civil airliner consisting of a double-bubble fuselage wedded to a 126ft span wing with tip tanks. Three BOAC captains had flown in the Victor by the end of 1953 and in 1955 the HP97 was revised around the Victor Mk 2 wing. In a forecast written by Godfrey Lee, the HP97 was to have had an all-up weight of 200,000lb, sufficient performance to transport 130 tourist seats plus 6,000lb of freight between New York and London at a cruising speed of 500kt, a cruising altitude of 45,000ft, and a direct operating cost of 0.90d per passenger mile.

In 1956 the HP97 was tendered to BOAC as a British alternative to the Boeing 707, yet Charles Joy admits with hindsight that 'the HP97 didn't stand a chance. There were so many factors bound

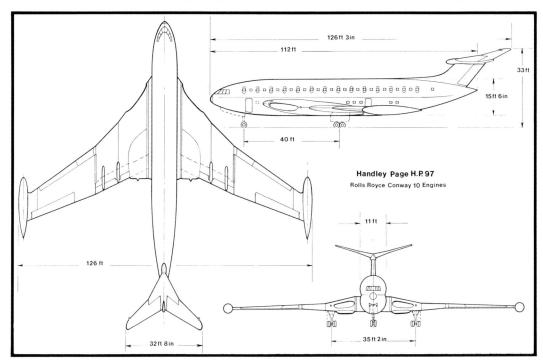

Handley Page H.P. 97
Rolls Royce Conway 10 Engines

up with the military requirement that conditioned its layout. Though we argued forcibly that all this Victor research should be employed on the civil side, there were a great many compromises that would have had to have been accepted.'

A military version of the HP97 was then offered to the RAAF as the HP97A but to no avail. Then in May 1958, there followed a much more viable proposition — a new circular-section pressurised transport, the HP111, employing many components common to the Victor B2 plus others proposed for the Victor B Phase 3. Its span had grown to 130ft including tip tanks, and a double-deck arrangement in the circular fuselage provided six-abreast aft-facing seats for 145 troops on the upper deck and five-abreast for 55 below. Alternatively, while still retaining 30 seats above and forward of the wing, the upper deck could be lowered by two hoists to provide space for a complete Twin Pioneer or five ¼-ton Army trucks loaded through rear clam-shell doors. Whether it be nearly 13 tons of military equipment or 200 troops, the HP111 promised to carry them over a still-air range of 3,300nm.

The Conway-engined 'Treble One' was a unique military transport in that it combined a long-range cruising speed of 10 miles a minute with a tactical ability to land at 180,000lb on 1,000yd grass airstrips. Reggie Stafford announced in August 1958 that it could be produced relatively quickly and cheaply such that if an order was placed that

year, the HP111 could be in service by the end of 1962. He illustrated the aircraft's value to the RAF by referring to a recent Cyprus airlift where 3,500 men and over 90 tons of freight had been ferried out from Britain by 45 aircraft in five days. The same task, said Stafford, could have been completed by six HP111s in two days.

The HP111 was tendered to the RAF in 1958, and later a civil HP111C, capable of carrying 145 passengers on the upper deck with a baggage and cargo hold below, was offered to BOAC. By this time the RAF had issued an Operational Requirement for a military transport and it is believed that the Air Staff selected the HP111 as the aircraft they wanted. However, the contract was eventually awarded to another early 'wide body', the Shorts Belfast. The need for employment in Northern Ireland might explain why, two weeks before the 1959 General Election, it was announced that the HP111 had been rejected in favour of an aircraft that would carry 50 less troops 150-200kt slower. The loss of a military order meant the end of civil hopes as well; in Godfrey Lee's opinion, 'our near miss in 1959 with the HP111 was one of the crucial misfortunes suffered by Handley Page'.

11

Victor Twilight

Early in 1969, No 543 Squadron's SR2s were ferried in turn to Radlett for major inspection before returning to Wyton in a new gloss polyurethane camouflage. Then in May, No 543 Squadron entered two Victors and their crews in the *Daily Mail* transatlantic air race commemorating the 50th anniversary of Alcock and Brown's first direct crossing from Newfoundland to Ireland. The aim was to achieve the fastest time between the top of the GPO Tower in London and the top of the Empire State Building in New York, and XL161, aided by prevailing winds, enabled a fleet-footed co-pilot to make the eastbound journey in 5hr 49min 28sec.

Marham tankers assisted a RN Phantom to make the fastest time of all, and there were to be many other demonstrations of the value of what was now termed air-to-air refuelling (AAR). During the 1974 Cyprus emergency, for example, the commander of the UN peace-keeping force made an urgent request for RAF support. Taking-off at 2hr notice from Britain on the night of 24 July, 12 Phantoms were on 10min standby in Akrotiri by first light on 25 July thanks to Victor assistance.

But although K1 and K1A Victors could transfer their own weight in fuel, their performance was restricted by their Sapphire engines. More powerful B2Rs made redundant by the disbandment of the Wittering Wing were natural successors because they could add two drop-tanks worth of fuel to every towline and would be less limited when operating out of hot-and-high airfields.

The Victor K2 conversion contract was technically agreed with Handley Page in October 1969 but it was initially limited to design and feasibility studies much to Radlett's financial chagrin. In an effort to maintain its independence after Sir Frederick's death, Handley Page had decided in August 1965 to concentrate on a short-haul turboprop passenger transport called the HP137 Jetstream. Orders were not slow in coming, particularly from across the Atlantic, but the prototype and early production aircraft were somewhat overweight and by the end of 1968 the company had spent £5½ million on development.

This drain on finances was not eased by a slump in the aviation market. Buyers held back from parting with ready cash until the Jetstream reached its brochure performance, and the only immediate way of achieving this was to install more powerful engines which demanded more money and time.

'We felt sure', said Godfrey Lee, 'that we who had done the Victor could quickly do a small 300mph twin turboprop aeroplane. I think we all underestimated the difficulties of the task we had undertaken.' Thus by the time full certification was in sight in August 1969, the Jetstream development bill had topped £13 million representing a break-even requirement of 1,000 sales instead of the original 400. Creditors started asking for cash instead of extending credit, and for a company with all its cash tied up on the shop floor, the only solution was to go into voluntary liquidation on 8 August. A rescue operation was mounted with American money but it was very dependent on the Victor 2 tanker conversion contract being confirmed. 'We could have survived with £1½ million from the Ministry of Defence', said Reggie Stafford, but the tanker lifeline was never thrown and on 2 March 1970 employees arriving at Radlett were sent home, apart from a skeleton staff to provide product support for RAF Victors.

Within two months the Victor K2 contract was awarded to Hawker Siddeley, and between April and July the 21 Victors mothballed at Radlett, plus the veteran trials B1 XA922, were transferred to the old Avro factory at Woodford that had sired the Vulcan. Sir Frederick must have turned in his grave.

The prototype K2, XL231, first flew from Woodford on 1 March 1972 but it did not have its internal structure completely updated. Still in its Wittering colours, XL231 was destined initially for Boscombe where close circuit TV was installed to monitor the behaviour of refuelling equipment in flight: only later was it reworked to the full K2 production standard.

The conversion contract specifically stated that there was to be no reversionary bomber role so out went all the Blue Steel and free-fall weapons equipment, the Window and ECM fit apart from the Blue Saga passive warning receiver, and all

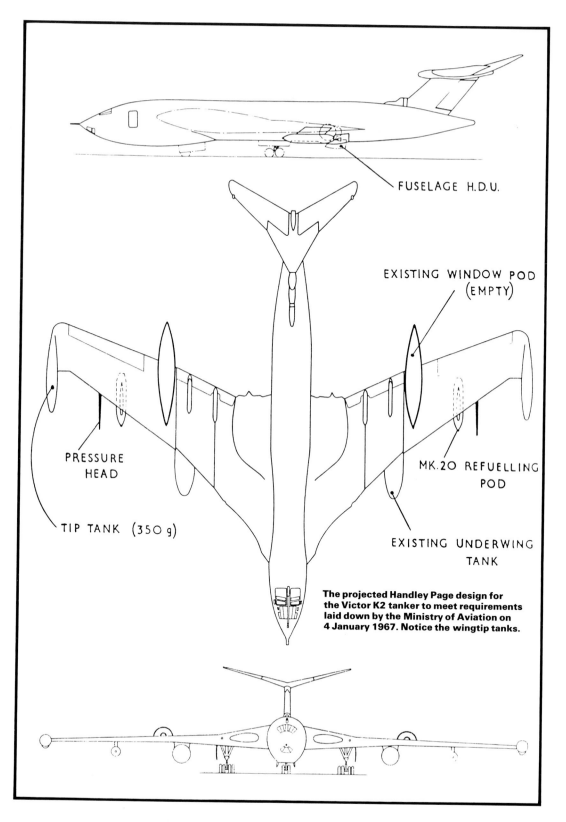

FUSELAGE H.D.U.

EXISTING WINDOW POD
(EMPTY)

PRESSURE
HEAD

MK.20 REFUELLING
POD

TIP TANK (350 g)

EXISTING UNDERWING
TANK

**The projected Handley Page design for
the Victor K2 tanker to meet requirements
laid down by the Ministry of Aviation on
4 January 1967. Notice the wingtip tanks.**

electrical cable looms and other accessories that were superfluous to in-flight refuelling. Few external changes were immediately apparent. The most obvious was the Mk 17 HDU in the bomb bay plus underwing Mk 20B refuelling pods alongside

the existing drop tanks; however, the latter were no longer jettisonable. A keener eye would have detected a new tail cone, incorporating a fuel jettison facility, and 1½ft was taken off each wing-tip (making a total span of 117ft) to reduce wing fatigue. Handley Page had intended to add small 350gal capacity tip tanks to act as bob weights, but despite funding completion of this design study, Hawker Siddeley finally opted for the alternative method of decreasing wing loads by reducing span to move the centre of pressure inboard.

Structural refurbishment inside the wing also concentrated on known fatigue areas, especially around the mainplane attachment, to restore the airframe fatigue index to zero. Zinc-free DTD 5104 was used on the forgings in place of DTD 683, and L73 in lieu of DTD 687 for the skins. Riveting replaced spot-welding in the new sandwich skin

Above:
XL233, the second Victor K2 conversion by Hawker Siddeley, with all hoses trailing.

Above right:
A No 57 Squadron line-up at Marham.

parts and the gauge of the skins and corrugations was increased. Each K2 emerged from Woodford with a design life of 14 years free from fatigue problems.

Inside the cockpit the fuel control panel was completely redesigned to cope with 127,000lb of fuel, and the pilots' flying instrumentation panels were updated and finished in a chic shade of grey. Among rear cabin improvements was the installation of a new Smiths Industries' rear view periscope incorporating a swivelling eyepiece to see all customers.

The first production K2 to enter service, XL233, was flown to join No 232 OCU at Marham on 8 May 1974. Normal maximum take-off weight was 223,000lb but when operationally essential, weight could be increased to 238,000lb. There was a proposal to resurrect rocket-assisted take-off for such heavy loads, but nothing came of this though it was recognised that overweight operations would reduce the structural strength reserve.

Twenty-eight Victor 2s were initially earmarked for conversion to K2s, beginning with the 21 B2Rs. The remainder were to have come from No 543 Squadron, which duly disbanded on 31 May 1974 when its radar reconnaissance role was taken over by No 27 Squadron Vulcans. A Victor Flight of four aircraft was kept in being at Wyton until 30 May 1975 to monitor French nuclear tests in the Pacific, but in the end this made no difference because financial constraints eventually allowed only 24 Victors to be modified to K2s. As this number was regarded as only sufficient to re-equip No 55 and No 57 Squadrons plus No 232 OCU, the doyen of flight refuellers, No 214 Squadron, had to be disbanded on 28 January 1977 when its K1s and K1As were phased out.

From now on the Marham Wing stabilised into an almost daily routine of supporting the RAF fighter force in its defence of UK airspace. For air defence Lightnings and Phantoms flying hundreds of miles offshore, loiter time was of major importance and their hard points were better used for weapons than drop tanks. Once it was appreciated that time on station could be tripled without affecting crew fatigue, Victor tankers became a valued 'force multiplier'.

Life was enlivened by regular 'trails' escorting attack aircraft to North America to take part in 'Red Flag' exercises, or to Cyprus for annual range firing practice, but it would be wrong to imply that tanking life was always easy. For instance on 24 March 1975, a refuelling Buccaneer struck the port tailplane of K1A XH618, damaging it so much that the whole Victor tailplane assembly broke off. XH618 plummeted immediately and only the captain managed to overcome the crushing 'g' forces and eject.

So might the Victor force have remained largely outside the public eye had not Argentina invaded the Falkland Islands on 2 April 1982. It was clear from the start of Operation 'Corporate' that the Victor tanker fleet would have an important role to play in any attempt to reassert British sovereignty. Yet despite manpower support from No 232 OCU, there were less than two dozen Victor K2s available to supplement South Atlantic operations, and the air defence of the UK could not be neglected. So even those crews recently arrived at Marham had to be capable of carrying out the most demanding aspect of their craft, mid-air refuelling of the tankers themselves by day or night. The latest navigation equipment was also fitted for very long flights over water together with an improvised camera fit in some K2 noses.

By 18 April, No 55 and 57 Squadrons were in a position to detach six Victors to Wideawake, the mid-Atlantic staging airfield on Ascension Island. Some 2,850 miles away lay South Georgia, the first objective to be recovered from Argentina. But

before a landing could take place, the British had to know whether the Argentinian Navy was in the area in strength. The reconnaissance Vulcans of No 27 Squadron having disbanded a month

No 57 Squadron prepares to refuel No 55 Squadron during long-range refuelling training.

previously, Victor tankers were the only aircraft immediately available and suitable for carrying out maritime radar reconnaissance over the vast distances involved.

At 02.50hrs local time on 20 April, four fully-laden tankers took off from Wideawake at 1min intervals to support reconnaissance Victor XL192 captained by Sqn Ldr John Elliott, formerly of No 543 Squadron. About 1,000 miles south of Ascension, two Victors gave all their spare fuel to the other pair and then returned to base. Two hours and a further 1,000 miles later, another refuelling took place and then the Elliott crew were on their own.

Arriving off the northeast tip of South Georgia at dawn, XL192 descended from 43,000ft to 18,000ft so that Nav Radar Sqn Ldr A. I. B. Beedie could scan all around for 'blips' on his H2S.

Left:
Looking none the worse with the passage of time, Johnny Allam (left) and Godfrey Lee (right) together with a Victor K2 at Marham in 1980. The bulge at the front of the Victor's nose, just above the artificial feel pitot intake, was the now redundant aerial for the auto-landing system.

The search took just over 90min and covered an area of more than 150,000sq miles — the equivalent of the whole of the British Isles — before the Victor returned to Ascension late in the afternoon courtesy of another four tankers. Having been airborne for 14hr 45min and covered about 6,500nm, the Elliott crew brought back radar prints to show that there were no warships of any size in the area and that the northern approaches were iceberg free. In so doing, both they and XL192 captured the record for the longest-ranging operational reconnaissance mission to date.

Two further air-refuelled Victor maritime radar reconnaissance missions were flown before this task was handed over to RAF Nimrods with their more advanced sensors. The delay in employing these specialist aircraft was caused by the need to modify Nimrods, and train their crews, so that they too could refuel in the air. Two 'fill-ups' were required on each outbound Nimrod leg from Ascension, and one more during the return. This alone did not account for the number of support Victors required but rather it was always necessary, over such great distances, to refuel the refuellers. Thus when the first Vulcan bombing mission was mounted against Port Stanley airfield early in the morning of 1 May, this single operation

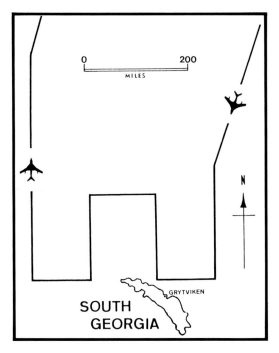

Above:
The search pattern flown by Sqn Ldr John Elliott and his No 55 Squadron crew during the radar reconnaissance off South Georgia on 20 April 1982.

SOUTH
GEORGIA

GRYTVIKEN

0   200
MILES

N

called for no fewer than 11 Victor support sorties outbound plus a further five at the rendezvous (RV) point on the return. The RAF had not flown such a co-ordinated, big aircraft operation since World War 2, and even then no Bomber Command raid had equated to a flight from England to bomb Chicago airport and back. More than 80 aircrew gathered for the pre-flight briefing in a flapping tent at Wideawake for what was basically to be a Victor operation launching a stand-off Vulcan at the very end.

A primary and a reserve Vulcan took off on the operation codenamed 'Black Buck 1'; in the event, the primary aircraft would not pressurise in the climb so the secondary crew took over the mantle. Ahead of them at 1min intervals had roared off 11 Victor tankers of which two were reserves: one was needed because a Victor crew found that they could not wind out their HDU, but the second was able to return to base.

In the van of the 'Black Buck' formation was the 'tanker lead' who was always an experienced Victor captain. The first fuel transfer, supervised by tanker leader Sqn Ldr Mike Todd, took place about 1¾hr after take-off some 840 miles south of Ascension. Four Victors topped up the tanks of four others and then turned back; this 'cascade' system was repeated a number of times thereafter until only one Victor remained with the bomber.

Unfortunately, after 5½hr in the air, events 2,750 miles south of Ascension were not going to plan. For a start, the Vulcan's fuel consumption was considerably greater than forecast because it was operating at higher than normal weights and the recently fitted underwing ECM pod was causing extra drag. In addition, because the heavily laden Victors could not reach the optimum Vulcan operating height, the bomber had to keep descending to a less economical level to refuel.

To cap it all, after topping up the Vulcan's tanks once more, Sqn Ldr Bob Tuxford in XL189 found that he had to refuel the remaining Victor right over the top of violent storm clouds. Flt Lt Steve Biglands' Victor (XH669) closed in behind Tuxford's only to see the hose and basket dancing up and down by about 20ft. After some superb flying, Biglands managed to get his probe into the drogue only to suffer a broken probe before transfer was complete. There was nothing for it but for Tuxford and Biglands to change places and for Tuxford to take back the fuel he had just given away plus sufficient for the Vulcan to reach Port Stanley. The skies cleared to make this possible, but the airborne minuet had taken the penultimate Victor well south of where it should have turned back. XH669 therefore not only had to fly further to get home, but Biglands also had to retain a reasonable reserve because his broken probe prevented him from taking on any more fuel.

Thus when the Vulcan refuelled for the last time before descending towards its target just over an hour away, it was still some 6,000lb short when Tuxford flashed his red lights to indicate that the transfer was over. He had sacrificed so much before peeling away and heading north that he would need a tank-up himself if XL189 was not to ditch 400 miles south of Ascension.

The second part of the mission was to get all the aircraft safely back to Wideawake. The first four Victors to return were so short of fuel that they had to land in stream, thereby putting all that good short landing practise with the brake chute to good use. For the Tuxford crew it was a longer, drier journey home. 'We discussed a lot of things, including the practical aspects of bailing out of a Victor into the sea — you could not hope to ditch it, the aircraft is the wrong shape. We had our radar on to see if there were any ships in the area, but in fact there was none in the right place.'

Fortunately Tuxford was able to rendezvous with one of the first wave tankers that had been hurriedly turned round and sent to meet him, while an equally apprehensive Vulcan crew arrived at their first tanking point off the coast of Brazil critically short of fuel. They need not have worried because, exactly to plan, the white underside of another of the first wave Victors swung into position. It was, in the words of the Vulcan

Above:
A receiver's-eye view of the HDU. Calm nerves were crucial in this close formation position.

captain, 'the most beautiful sight in the world'. For his selfless efforts, Bob Tuxford was awarded the AFC.

With the first Vulcan raid judged to be a success, 'Black Buck 2' was launched late in the evening of 3 May. The lessons of two days earlier had been taken to heart and instead of one huge formation going south, shedding tankers like leaves off a tree, 'Black Buck 2' consisted of two smaller groups. The first contained the Vulcan and its immediate replenishers, who took the bomber two-thirds of the way to Port Stanley before the last Victor turned back. The second tanker wave took off about 5min after the first, and they flew at a slightly greater height and speed so that they caught up well down the route. Their eventual task was to fill a single Victor full of fuel so that it could replenish the Vulcan immediately prior to its descent towards the target. In the words of the captain of the Vulcan concerned, the tanker plan 'worked like magic; people were throwing fuel at us from every direction'.

Victors would escort a Vulcan down to Port Stanley on four more occasions, and only one of these missions had to be aborted when, just before the penultimate 'prod', two Victors were unable to pass fuel to each other because of a failure in the donor's HDU. By the last Vulcan raid on 12 June,

Right:
The 'Black Buck 1' tanker plan.

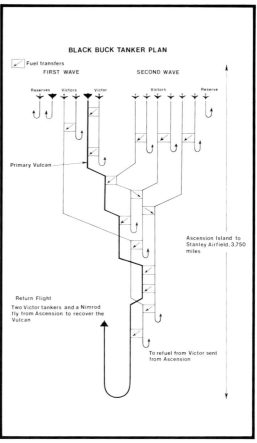

BLACK BUCK TANKER PLAN

Fuel transfers

FIRST WAVE   SECOND WAVE

Reserves Victors Victor   Victors   Reserve

Primary Vulcan

Ascension Island to
Stanley Airfield, 3,750
miles

Return Flight
Two Victor tankers and a Nimrod
fly from Ascension to recover the
Vulcan

To refuel from Victor sent
from Ascension

Victor crews had refined their performance to such an extent that the bomber captain described the sortie as 'almost old hat'.

But Victors and their crews were 'extending' other types besides the Vulcan. Nimrods searched the sea for diesel submarines, crucial Harrier replacements were flown out to reinforce the invading Task Force, and Hercules transports eventually dropped high-priority supplies over a free but unusable Port Stanley airfield, all courtesy of the ubiquitous Victor.

The scale of air-refuelling operations from Ascension Island during 'Corporate' operations was such that tanker aircrews were regularly flying up to 120hr a month, much of it at night or in unpredictable weather conditions. Peacetime aircraft flying rates were trebled and, frequently, 15 out of the 16 Victors at Wideawake were needed to meet the daily tasking. Over a two-month period these tankers flew some 3,000hr on 530 combat missions, giving away 23 million pounds weight of fuel in the process. During the whole South Atlantic campaign, only three missions failed through malfunction of the Victor's refuelling equipment and none had to be cancelled as a result of tanker aircraft unserviceability. It was a remarkable record and in the words of AVM Michael Knight, AOC No 1 Group, in which the tankers now served, 'the outstanding performance of the ageing Victor and its crews was the very cornerstone of air operations in support of the Falklands Task Force'.

Victors continued to be heavily committed in the South Atlantic even when hostilities ended. Their task eased with the introduction of the Hercules tanker and the reopening of Port Stanley airfield, but it only ended on 10 June 1985 when the newly opened Mount Pleasant airfield was in a position to receive wide body jets.

Meanwhile back at Woodford, the old Radlett B2 fatigue specimen, consisting of a fuselage and mainplanes, was continuing the good work as the K2 specimen. Unfortunately, in November 1982 it revealed the old Wittering problem of serious cracks in both the port and starboard wing lower booms. The bottom boom was the most critical part of the wing structure being in torsion during flight, and by the time the cracks were found, propagation was too extensive to be arrested by repair. Major refurbishment was also discounted because it was more cost-effective to convert ex-civil airline VC10s and TriStars to the tanker role. The fuel transfer capacity of a TriStar being equal to that of about eight Victors, it was decided to set a maximum Victor fatigue life limit based on that of the specimen airframe and leave it at that.

Ironically, while Victor Conway engine problems dramatically reduced during the Falklands campaign, perhaps demonstrating the benefit of using machinery constantly, the high intensity of heavily-laden South Atlantic operations had taken its toll of Victor airframe life. 'Young' K2s, such as XL164 with only 1,626hr on the clock from new, were a rarity, and some of the others were rapidly

Above:
Landing back at Ascension Island. *Steve Millard*

a turbine disc. Consequently it was decided to retire the least sustainable aircraft and disband 232 OCU in April 1986 together with No 57 Squadron on 30 June. This left an enlarged No 55 Squadron with 10 aircraft plus five in-use reserves. They were converted to four-man crew operation during 1986 by the simple expedient of re-positioning the AAR controls in the AEO's left side plus removing one navigator's seat and mounting the other seat on rails so that it could slide sideways to cover both navigating stations. The remaining navigator, who probably felt he deserved double pay even though

ageing. The Victor force was also being eroded by accidents such as that to XL232 which was destroyed on 15 October 1982 following failure of

Below:
'Jaws'. XL190, with locally modified paint scheme, is seen at Marham just after returning from Ascension Island. The nosewheel door was missing because the aircraft was undergoing repair following failure of the nosewheel to lower before landing. *Steve Millard*

some of the Nav Radar's kit had been deleted, must have been comforted by the A&AEE reassurance that 'no safety or operation problems are encountered by aircrew within the 3rd and 99th percentile anthropometric range'.

Victor tankers soldiered on operationally until 15 October 1993, when No 55 Squadron disbanded. Of the seven remaining Victor tankers, three went to fire dumps, one had its nose cut off for the RAF Museum, and three went to be cared for at Bruntingsthorpe, Cosford and Elvington. The last Victor flight took place on 30 November 1993 when XH672 flew with Johnny Allam on board. Forty years had elapsed between first prototype flight to snd demise. Set against any criteria, that was a remarkable achievement for a remarkable aeroplane.

Right:
A Victor K2 of No 57 Squadron in its latest 'low conspicuity' hemp finish. *Edward Davies*

Bottom left:
When a fully-laden tanker catches fire, it burns. This is all that remains of XL232 after No 3 engine exploded as the brakes were released on 15 October 1982. Miraculously, all crew members escaped without injury.

Bottom right:
The bitter end: XL513 lies forlorn after catching fire during take-off from Marham on 28 September 1976.

Bottom far right:
A Victor tanker replenishes its successor in the RAF bomber inventory, the Tornado GR1. *Edward Davies*

Appendices

Victor Family Tree

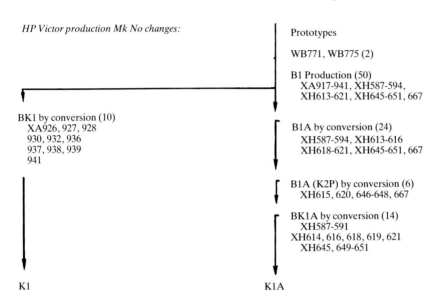

HP Victor production Mk No changes:

Prototypes

WB771, WB775 (2)

B1 Production (50)
    XA917-941, XH587-594,
    XH613-621, XH645-651, 667

BK1 by conversion (10)
    XA926, 927, 928
    930, 932, 936
    937, 938, 939
    941

B1A by conversion (24)
    XH587-594, XH613-616
    XH618-621, XH645-651, 667

B1A (K2P) by conversion (6)
    XH615, 620, 646-648, 667

BK1A by conversion (14)
    XH587-591
    XH614, 616, 618, 619, 621
    XH645, 649-651

K1

K1A

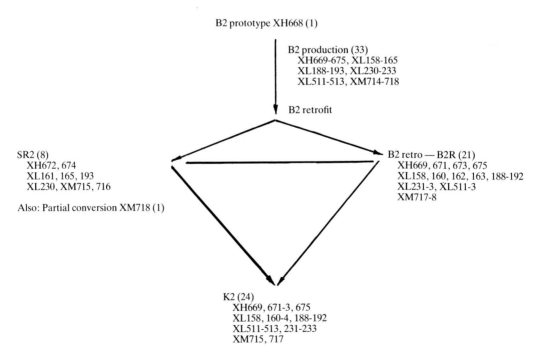

B2 prototype XH668 (1)

B2 production (33)
    XH669-675, XL158-165
    XL188-193, XL230-233
    XL511-513, XM714-718

B2 retrofit

SR2 (8)
    XH672, 674
    XL161, 165, 193
    XL230, XM715, 716

Also: Partial conversion XM718 (1)

B2 retro — B2R (21)
    XH669, 671, 673, 675
    XL158, 160, 162, 163, 188-192
    XL231-3, XL511-3
    XM717-8

K2 (24)
    XH669, 671-3, 675
    XL158, 160-4, 188-192
    XL511-513, 231-233
    XM715, 717

With acknowledgements to Roger Brooks

— Victor Production

Prototypes

Contract 6/Acft/1875/CB6(a) dated 28 April 1948
WB771. First flew 24/12/52; flight trials; crashed Cranfield 14/7/53.
WB775. First flew 11/9/53; flight trials; dismantled 1959; P&EE, Foulness, 1961.

B1 and B1A

Contract 6/Acft/8441/CB6(a) dated June 1952 — 25 delivered
1. XA917. Aw C, 8/2/56; A&AEE trials, 1/4/56; dismantled after crash landing at Radlett, 1/64, nose to serve as crew drill trainer at Marham.
2. XA918. Aw C, 29/3/56; A&AEE, 29/3/56; transferred to C(A), 23/6/56; prototype K1 conversion; SOC, 7/70.
3. XA919. Conference aircraft; Aw C, 25/3/57; A&AEE, 19/9/57, flying accident, 3/9/59; RAF Locking for instructional purposes, 16/5/61; Radlett fatigue and structure ground rig, 9/66.
4. XA920. Aw C, 6/56; A&AEE, 6/56; C(A), 20/3/57; P&EE Shoeburyness, 25/9/63.
5. XA921. Aw C, 12/7/56; A&AEE, 12/6/56; C(A), 14/3/57; returned to RAF disposal, 14/10/62; SOC, 17/10/64.
6. XA922. Aw C, 29/11/57; A&AEE, 29/11/57; C(A), 19/4/58; MoA, 11/60; HS for ground trials, 8/4/70; Cosford by Aug 73; scrapped 74.
7. XA923. Aw C, 31/1/58; 232 OCU, 4/2/58; RRF 14/4/58; 232 OCU, 16/10/61; HP, 22/10/63; Cosford for instructional purposes, 27/5/64; Cosford Museum 74-75; scrapped Mar 85
8. XA924. Aw C, 24/1/58; 232 OCU, 27/1/58; RRF, 21/3/58; 232 OCU, 9/10/61; HP, 24/7/62; 232 OCU, 11/2/63; 10 Sqn, 28/6/63; St Athan for instructional purposes, 20/4/64; scrapped by 69.
9. XA925. Aw C, 28/2/58; 232 OCU, 4/3/58; RRF, 16/4/58; 232 OCU, 15/9/61; HP, 3/9/62; 15 Sqn, 26/6/63; MoA, 20/4/64; dismantled Radlett, 65; SOC, 7/66.
10. XA926. Aw C, 14/3/58; 232 OCU, 17/3/58; HP for conversion to K1, 17/9/64; 57 Sqn, 23/3/66; 55 Sqn, 3/6/74; 57 Sqn, 17/6/74; St Athan, 26/5/76; SOC, 22/11/76.
11. XA927. Aw C, 15/4/58; 10 Sqn, 15/4/58; 15 Sqn, 20/5/64; HP for conv K1, 17/9/64; 214 Sqn, 4/10/66; SOC St Athan, 1/2/77.
12. XA928. Aw C, 25/3/57; A&AEE, 29/3/57; 10 Sqn, 5/5/58; HP for conv K1, 10/9/64; 57 Sqn, 2/3/66; 214 Sqn, 9/8/76; St Athan, 16/12/76.
13. XA929. Aw C, 23/6/58; 10 Sqn, 23/6/58; 232 OCU, 8/4/59; 10 Sqn, 6/6/60; flying accident — on take-off Akrotiri, 16/6/62; SOC, 2/8/62.
14. XA930. Aw C, 30/9/57; A&AEE, 9/10/57; HP, 23/6/61; 10 Sqn, 30/9/63; 232 OCU, 15/9/64; Honington Wg, 18/3/65; 57 Sqn, 1/11/65; HP for conv K1, 10/5/66; 55 Sqn, 3/4/67; 214 Sqn, 1/8/67; St Athan, 9/7/74; SOC, 17/4/75.
15. XA931. Aw C, 28/11/57; 232 OCU, 28/11/57; 10 Sqn, 14/12/61; 232 OCU, 30/8/63; St Athan, 26/6/64; SOC, 30/4/74.
16. XA932. Aw C, 11/2/58; 232 OCU, 13/2/58; 10 Sqn, 29/7/59; MoA, 6/3/64; HP for conv K1, 2/9/66; 214 Sqn, 11/8/66; Marham for ground instructional purposes,

2/2/77 static display; scrapped Oct 86.
17. XA933. Aw C, 2/58; 232 OCU, 3/3/58; flying accident — wheels-up landing Waddington, 24/2/59; HP, 27/3/62; MoA (low-level radar trials), 22/5/64; Honington Wg, 29/4/65; 55 Sqn, 1/12/65; TTF, 23/8/66; St Athan, 26/4/67; SOC, 1/10/71.
18. XA934. Aw C, 21/3/58; 232 OCU, 25/3/58; flying accident — engine failure near Gaydon, 2/10/62; SOC, 3/10/62.
19. XA935. Aw C, 2/4/58; 10 Sqn, 9/4/58; 232 OCU, 29/10/58; RRF, 11/5/59; 15 Sqn, 1/3/60; 232 OCU, 9/5/61; 10 Sqn, 1/11/61; 232 OCU, 14/12/61; St Athan, 17/6/64; SOC, 30/4/74.
20. XA936. Aw C, 23/5/58; 10 Sqn, 28/5/58; 232 OCU, 27/2/59; HP for conv K1, 11/1/65; 214 Sqn, 29/11/66; St Athan, 23/6/76; SOC, 20/9/76.
21. XA937. Aw C, 31/5/58; 10 Sqn, 4/6/58; 15 Sqn, 2/3/64; HP for conv first K1, 30/4/64; MoA, 26/11/65; 57 Sqn, 15/2/66; 214 Sqn, 3/10/66; SOC St Athan, 7/2/77; P&EE, Foulness, 79.
22. XA938. Aw C, 22/7/58; 10 Sqn, 28/7/58; 15 Sqn, 2/3/64; HP for conv K1, 12/10/64; 214 Sqn, 28/9/66; MOD(PE), 30/9/76; SOC, 78; P&EE, Foulness, 79.
23. XA939. Aw C, 27/8/58; 10 Sqn, 27/8/58; 15 Sqn, 2/3/64; HP for conv K1, 8/10/64; MoA, 5/7/66; 214 Sqn, 22/11/66; SOC Catterick, 29/3/76.
24. XA940. Aw C, 9/9/58; 10 Sqn, 10/9/58; flying accident — undercarriage failed to lock down, 19/12/61; 232 OCU, 7/11/62; 10 Sqn, 11/1/63; 15 Sqn, 2/3/64; 232 OCU, 15/10/64; Honington Wg, 9/3/65; 57 Sqn, 1/12/65; TTF, 1/1/67; Min Tech, 8/6/67; St Athan, 25/7/68; SOC, 31/8/73; nose to Marham, May 74.
25. XA941. Aw C, 11/9/58; 15 Sqn, 17/9/58; 10 Sqn, 25/1/59; 55 Sqn, 8/9/60; 232 OCU, 23/3/61; 10 Sqn, 3/9/63; 15 Sqn, 2/3/64; flying accident — centre-line closure, 2/9/64; Honington Wg, 2/2/65; HP, 13/5/65; MoA, 27/10/65; HP for conv K1, 20/12/65; 214 Sqn, 19/12/66; St Athan, 15/8/74; SOC, 22/11/74.

Contract 6/Ac ft/11303/CB6(a) dated May 1955 — 25 delivered
26. XH587. Aw C, 17/10/58; 15 Sqn, 17/10/58; HP for ECM trials and conv B1A, 6/4/61; 15 Sqn, 16/8/62; HP for conv K1A, 6/10/64; 57 Sqn, 29/4/66; St Athan, 16/7/74; SOC, 17/4/75; scrapped.
27. XH588. Aw C, 28/10/58; 15 Sqn, 30/10/58; HP for conv B1A, 2/8/61; 55 Sqn, 1/6/62; Honington Wg; HP for conv K1A, 25/11/65; 214 Sqn, 7/12/66; 55 Sqn, 1/8/67; 57 Sqn, 23/6/75; Machrihanish FF, 30/7/75.
28. XH589. Aw C, 21/11/58; 15 Sqn, 1/12/58; HP for conv B1A, 6/11/61; 55 Sqn, 11/6/62; Honington Wg; TTF, 12/7/65; HP for conv K1A, 12/7/66; 55 Sqn, 28/4/67; 57 Sqn, 11/3/74; 55 Sqn, 25/3/74; 214 Sqn, 25/6/75; St Athan, 6/5/76; St Athan FF, 9/7/76.
29. XH590. Aw C, 26/11/58; 15 Sqn, 1/12/58; HP for conv B1A, 3/10/61; 57 Sqn, 14/9/62; HP for conv K1A, 1/12/65; 55 Sqn, 12/1/67; 57 Sqn, 25/2/74; 55 Sqn, 11/3/74; Manston FF, 3/7/75.
30. XH591. Aw C, 7/1/59; 15 Sqn, 20/1/59; HP for conv B1A, 16/1/62; 55 Sqn, 6/2/63; Honington Wg; 57 Sqn, 1/12/65; HP for conv K1A, 13/7/66; 55 Sqn, 2/5/67; Min Tech, 17/9/68; 55 Sqn, 24/11/69; 57 Sqn, 23/6/75;

214 Sqn, 2/6/76; SOC St Athan, 5/11/76.
31. XH592. Aw C, 31/12/58; 15 Sqn, 2/2/59; HP for conv B1A, 1/9/61; Honington Wg, 5/7/62; 232 OCU, 11/3/65; TTF, 23/6/65; flying accident — bomb door came off in flight, 15/1/68; TTF/232 OCU, 13/8/68; Cosford for ground instruction, 16/10/74; Cosford Museum, 13/12/83.
32. XH593. Aw C, 26/1/59; 15 Sqn; HP for conv B1A; Honington Wg; TTF/232 OCU; Cosford for instructional purposes, 16 Oct 74; SOC, 18/4/85.
33. XH594. Aw C, 31/1/59; 15 Sqn, 3/2/59; HP for conv B1A, 22/7/60; Honington Wg, 27/3/61; flying accident — in-flight refuelling pipe broke flooding cabin, 24/1/64; 232 OCU, 9/3/65; St Athan, 19/2/74; SOC, 31/5/74.
34. XH613. Aw C, 27/2/59; HP for conv to first B1A, 4/60; 15 Sqn, 18/7/60; flying accident — fuel failure to all four engines on Cottesmore approach, 14/6/62; SOC, 15/6/62.
35. XH614. Aw C, 18/3/59; 57 Sqn, 23/3/59; HP for conv B1A, 30/9/60; 55 Sqn, 28/4/61; Honington Wg; flying accident — centre-line closure, Tengah, 24/11/64; TTF, 18/8/65; HP for conv K1A, 6/10/66; 55 Sqn, 15/8/67; Min Tech, 26/9/67; 55 Sqn, 4/1/68; 214 Sqn, 25/2/74; 55 Sqn, 8/4/74; 214 Sqn, 23/6/75; SOC, St Athan, 7/9/76.
36. XH615. Aw C, 7/4/59; 232 OCU, 8/4/59; HP for conv B1A, 11/1/61; 10 Sqn, 29/6/61; Honington Wg, 6/10/64; HP for conv B1A (K2P), 10/3/65; 55 Sqn, 21/6/65; TTF/232 OCU, 16/3/67; Leeming FF, 4/10/74.
37. XH616. Aw C, 21/4/59; 57 Sqn, 23/4/59; HP for conv B1A, 6/4/61; 15 Sqn, 19/9/61; flying accident — cabin door came away, 24/10/62; 15 Sqn, 28/11/62; Honington Wg, 22/9/64; 232 OCU, 18/3/65; HP for conv K1A, 16/8/66; 57 Sqn, 13/6/67; SOC FF, 20/1/76.
38. XH617. Aw C, 19/5/59; 57 Sqn, 25/5/59; flying accident — No 4 alternator drive shaft bearing failed, Oakley, Norfolk, 19/7/60; SOC, 20/7/60.
39. XH618. Aw C, 3/6/59; retained by HP for conv B1A; 15 Sqn, 15/8/60; flying accident — brake fire while taxiing, 4/2/63; 15 Sqn, 4/3/63; MoA (low-level trials), 16/9/63; HP for conv K1A, 14/8/64; MoA, 12/1/66; 57 Sqn, 15/8/66; flying accident — collision with Buccaneer, 24/3/75; SOC, 24/3/75.
40. XH619. Aw C, 24/6/59; 57 Sqn, 25/6/59; HP for conv B1A, 28/11/60; 57 Sqn, 1/6/61; Honington Wg; 57 Sqn, 1/12/65; HP for conv K1A, 9/6/66; 55 Sqn, 12/4/67; 214 Sqn, 8/8/73; Marham FF, 30/6/75.
41. XH620. Aw C, 20/7/59; 57 Sqn, 21/7/59; flying accident — cabin door opened in flight, 16/10/59; HP for conv B1A, 19/4/61; 15 Sqn, 27/10/61; Honington Wg, 4/3/64; HP for conv first B1A (K2P), 11/2/65; 55 Sqn, 21/5/65; 57 Sqn, 1/5/67; TTF, 23/8/67; 57 Sqn, 25/10/67; 232 OCU, 10/9/73; 57 Sqn, 30/10/73; 55 Sqn, 20/5/74; 57 Sqn, 3/6/74; St Athan, 30/10/75; SOC, 24/6/76.
42. XH621. Aw C, 31/7/59; retained by HP for conv B1A; 57 Sqn, 27/9/60; Honington Wg; flying accident — bomb bay tank became detached and burst bomb bay open, 4/9/65; 57 Sqn, 24/9/65; HP for conv K1A, 6/10/65; 57 Sqn, 30/11/66; 214 Sqn, 2/6/76; St Athan, 3/12/74.
43. XH645. Aw C, 25/9/59; 57 Sqn, 28/9/59; HP for conv B1A, 27/1/61; 55 Sqn, 12/7/61; Honington Wg; HP for conv K1A, 1/12/65; 55 Sqn, 24/1/67; St Athan, 14/2/74; SOC, 9/9/74.
44. XH646. Aw C, 30/9/59; retained by HP for conv B1A; 55 Sqn, 24/10/60; Honington Wg; HP for conv B1A (K2P), 19/3/65; 55 Sqn, 8/9/65; TTF, 20/3/67; flying accident — collided with Canberra B(I)6 over Holt, Norfolk, 19/8/68; SOC, 20/8/68.
45. XH647. Aw C, 19/11/59; retained by HP for conv B1A; 57 Sqn, 29/11/60; Honington Wg; HP for conv B1A (K2P), 16/2/65; 55 Sqn, 3/6/65; TTF/232 OCU, 17/1/67; 214 Sqn, 8/7/74; 232 OCU, 29/7/74; 57 Sqn, 28/8/74; 232 OCU, 30/9/74; crash rescue training, Catterick, 25/11/74.
46. XH648. Aw C, 21/12/59; 57 Sqn, 22/12/59; HP for conv

B1A, 26/10/60; 15 Sqn, 12/5/61; Honington Wg, 6/4/64; HP for conv B1A (K2P), 18/2/65; 55 Sqn, 20/5/65; 57 Sqn, 23/6/75; Duxford Museum, 2/6/76.
47. XH649. Aw C, 8/1/60; retained by HP for conv B1A; 57 Sqn, 20/1/61; Honington Wg; HP for conv K1A, 5/11/64; 57 Sqn, 10/6/66; St Athan, 10/11/75; SOC, 27/7/76.
48. XH650. Aw C, 5/2/60; retained by HP for conv B1A; 55 Sqn, 14/1/61; Honington Wg; HP for conv K1A, 24/9/64; 55 Sqn, 23/2/67; 214 Sqn, 22/4/74; 55 Sqn, 20/5/74; 214 Sqn, 23/6/75; Manston FF, 12/2/76.
49. XH651. Aw C, 31/3/60; 57 Sqn, 1/4/60; HP for conv B1A, 13/2/61; 15 Sqn, 10/8/61; HP for conv K1A, 9/10/64; 57 Sqn, 13/7/66; 214 Sqn, 2/6/76, St Athan, 26/1/77.
50. XH667. Aw C, 31/3/60; retained by HP for conv B1A; 57 Sqn, 3/2/61; Honington Wg; HP for conv B1A (K2P), 11/2/65; 55 Sqn, 27/5/65; 214 Sqn, 1/4/67; Hal Far FF, 23/9/75.

Victor B2

Contract 6/Ac ft/11303/CB6(a) as amended February 1956 — eight delivered
51. XH668. Aw C, 3/6/59; flying accident over St Bride's Bay prior to C(A) release, 20/8/59.
52. XH669. Aw C, 22/12/59; A&AEE, 22/12/59; HP for conv B2R; Wittering Wg, 8/7/64; HP, 10/10/68; HS awaiting conv K2, 3/6/70; 57 Sqn, 20/1/77; 55 Sqn, 20/3/86.
53. XH670. Aw C, 22/12/59; MoA, 1/3/60; HS for spares recovery, 3/3/74; derelict by 79.
54. XH671. Conference aircraft; Aw C, 4/5/60; A&AEE 4/5/60 for NBS/ECM trials; HP for conv B2R; Wittering Wg, 20/3/64; HP, 8/1/69; HS awaiting conv K2, 9/4/70; 57 Sqn, 6/8/76; 55 Sqn, 8/9/80; 57 Sqn, 25/2/85; 55 Sqn, 25/6/86.
55. XH672. Aw C, 26/5/60; A&AEE 26/5/60 for engine and autopilot/auto landing trials; HP for conv SR2, 2/7/64; 543 Sqn, 13/8/65; HS for conv K2, 19/3/74; 57 Sqn, 24/5/78; 55 Sqn, 2/7/86.
56. XH673. Aw C, 1/9/60; MoA, 1/9/60; flying accident — hydraulic failure at Waddington, 5/12/60; HP for conv B2R, 12/4/62; 139 Sqn, 5/12/63; Wittering Wg, 28/6/65; HP, 10/10/68; HS awaiting conv K2, 4/6/70; 57 Sqn, 17/12/76; Marham display, 2/7/86.
57. XH674. Aw C, 1/9/60; MoA — Blue Steel development trials, 1/9/60; HP for conv SR2, 17/7/64; 543 Sqn, 17/9/65; Victor Flight, 24/5/74; Marham, 15/10/75; SOC, 22/6/76.
58. XH675. Aw C, 8/3/61; MoA — PR development trials, 8/3/61; HP for conv B2R, 1/1/63; 100 Sqn, 17/2/64; HP, 4/10/68; HS awaiting conv K2, 15/6/70; 57 Sqn, 30/3/77; 55 Sqn, 1/10/80.

Contract 6/Ac ft/123996/CB6(a) dated January 1956 (last three added by amendment on 27 February 1956) — 21 delivered
59. XL158. Aw C, 30/12/60; MoA, 30/12/60; HP for conv B2R, 1/6/62; 139 Sqn, 27/9/63; Wittering Wg, 31/5/65; HP, 8/11/68; HS awaiting conv K2, 6/5/70; 55 Sqn, 12/4/76; 57 Sqn, 7/6/76; 55 Sqn, 14/3/85.
60. XL159. Aw C, 20/2/61; A&AEE, 28/2/61; flying accident — stable stall near Newark, 23/3/62; SOC, 31/10/62.
61. XL160. Aw C, 26/1/61; MoA for Conway engine tests, 26/1/61; HP for conv B2R, 27/7/62; 100 Sqn, 16/1/64; Wittering Wg, 19/7/65; HP, 25/10/68; HS awaiting conv K2, 21/5/70, 55 Sqn, 22/9/75; 57 Sqn, 2/10/80; 55 Sqn, 12/8/85; 57 Sqn, 8/8/86; SOC, 2/7/86.
62. XL161. Aw C, 27/3/61; MoA — Blue Steel trials, 27/3/61; HP for conv SR2, 29/10/64; 543 Sqn, 25/4/66; HS conv K2, 4/4/74; 55 Sqn, 20/3/78.
63. XL162. Aw C, 5/5/61; MoA, 5/5/61; HP for conv B2R,

8/6/62; 139 Sqn, 22/8/63; Wittering Wg, 23/9/65; HP, 14/1/69; HS awaiting conv K2, 13/5/70; 57 Sqn, 13/9/76; 55 Sqn, 16/12/80; 57 Sqn, 1/7/85; 55 Sqn, 26/6/86.

64. XL163. Aw C, 21/1/62; 139 Sqn, 7/2/62; 100 Sqn, 4/7/63; HP for conv B2R, 6/12/63; Wittering Wg, 1/9/64; HP, 14/1/69; HS for conv K2, 20/5/70; 232 OCU, 4/10/74; 55 Sqn, 3/7/75; 57 Sqn, 7/6/76; 55 Sqn, 18/10/76; 57 Sqn, 16/12/80; 55 Sqn, 8/1/86; St Athan, 2/7/86; SOC, 29/9/86.

65. XL164. Aw C, 5/6/61; retained by HP as B2R prototype; MoA, 31/5/63; St Athan, 1/6/67; HS for conv K2, 28/10/72; 57 Sqn, 25/5/77; 55 Sqn, 30/7/81; 57 Sqn, 29/4/85; 55 Sqn, 25/6/86.

66. XL165. Aw C, 18/10/61; 232 OCU, 8/11/61; Wittering Wg, 31/10/62; MoA, 22/3/65; HP for conv as prototype SR2, 12/4/65; 543 Sqn, 7/2/66; MoA, 7/6/66; 543 Sqn, 13/1/67; Victor Flight 24/5/74; St Athan, 27/3/75; SOC, 30/10/75.

67. XL188. Aw C, 23/10/61; 232 OCU, 2/11/61; HP for conv B2R, 14/4/64; Wittering Wg, 2/3/65; Min Tech, 2/1/69; HS for conv K2, 29/4/71; 55 Sqn, 7/1/75; 57 Sqn, 10/6/83; 55 Sqn, 18/12/84.

68. XL189. Aw C, 4/8/61; 232 OCU, 16/12/61; HP for conv B2R, 20/2/64; Wittering Wg, 1/12/64; HP, 17/10/68; HS for conv K2, 16/4/70; MOD(PE), 17/12/73; 232 OCU, 8/1/75; 55 Sqn, 3/7/75; 57 Sqn, 8/9/80; 55 Sqn, 13/5/85; 57 Sqn, 20/3/86; SOC Waddington, 2/7/86.

69. XL190. Aw C, 14/9/61; 139 Sqn, 3/5/62; HP for conv B2R, 13/8/63; Wittering Wg, 28/4/64; HP, 14/1/69; HS for conv K2, 10/7/70; 232 OCU, 12/12/74; 55 Sqn, 8/12/75; 57 Sqn, 19/12/84; 55 Sqn, 4/2/85.

70. XL191. Aw C, 20/9/61; 139 Sqn, 14/3/62; HP for conv B2R, 1/10/63; Wittering Wg, 6/5/64; HP, 15/10/68; HS for conv K2, 29/5/70; 232 OCU, 15/7/74; 55 Sqn, 1/1/77; flying accident — Hamilton, Ontario, 19/6/86; SOC, 7/7/86.

71. XL192. Aw C, 26/2/62; 100 Sqn, 28/6/62; flying accident — cabin door blew off, 22/4/63; HP for conv B2R, 20/1/64; Wittering Wg, 23/11/64; HP 28/10/68; HS for conv K2, 23/6/70; 57 Sqn, 16/6/76; 55 Sqn, 1/7/86.

72. XL193. Aw C, 24/8/62; 100 Sqn, 30/8/62; 232 OCU, 6/6/64; HP for conv SR2, 17/8/64; 543 Sqn, 21/6/66; Victor Flight, 24/5/74; St Athan, 3/4/75; SOC, 10/11/75.

73. XL230. Aw C, 13/12/61; 232 OCU, 21/12/61; HP for conv SR2, 28/5/64; 543 Sqn, 18/5/65; flying accident — control lost during roller landing, Wyton, 10/5/73; SOC, 10/5/73.

74. XL231. Aw C, 31/1/62; 139 Sqn, 1/2/62; HP for conv B2R, 8/11/63; Wittering Wg, 20/7/64; HP, 8/1/69; HS, 28/4/70; Min Tech, 21/7/70; HS for conv K2, 23/1/74; 57 Sqn, 11/7/77; 55 Sqn, 19/7/85; 57 Sqn, 12/8/85; 55 Sqn, 2/7/86.

75. XL232. Aw C, 9/3/62; 139 Sqn; HP for conv B2R;

Wittering Wg; HS for conv K2 18/11/74; RAE Bedford, 18/6/75; 232 OCU, 3/76; 55 Sqn, 6/78; 57 Sqn; flying accident — failure of turbine disc, 15/10/82; SOC, 16/10/82.

76. XL233. Aw C, 11/4/62; MoA, 4/4/62; HP for conv B2R, 25/7/63; Wittering Wg, 10/4/64; HP, 8/1/69; HS for conv K2, 22/4/70; 232 OCU, 7/5/74; 55 Sqn, 1/1/77; St Athan, 31/7/86.

77. XL511. Aw C, 14/5/62; Conv B2R; 139 Sqn, 26/7/63; Wittering Wg, 31/5/65; HP, 5/11/68; HS for conv K2, 1/7/70; 55 Sqn, 7/7/75; 57 Sqn, 1/7/85; 55 Sqn, 4/11/85; 57 Sqn, 29/1/86; Marham FF, 2/7/86.

78. XL512. Aw C, 29/6/62; retained by HP for conv B2R; 139 Sqn, 8/11/63; Wittering Wg, 17/9/64; HP, 2/1/69; Min Tech, 22/12/69; HS for conv K2, 25/6/70; 55 Sqn, 13/2/76; 57 Sqn, 7/6/76; 55 Sqn, 12/3/85.

79. XL513. Aw C, 31/8/62; retained by HP for conv B2R; 139 Sqn, 30/12/63; Wittering Wg, 20/1/65; flying accident — undercarriage failure at Manston, 8/1/68; HP, 2/10/68; HS for conv K2, 17/7/70; 55 Sqn, 21/3/75; flying accident — caught fire after aborting on take-off at Marham, 28/9/76; SOC, 28/9/76.

Contract 6/Ac ft/15566/CB6 — 5 delivered

80. XM714. Aw C, 20/11/62; 100 Sqn, 21/11/62; flying accident — stalled after take-off over Barnack, 20/3/63; SOC, 21/3/63.

81. XM715. Aw C, 31/12/62; 100 Sqn, 4/5/63; 232 OCU, 11/4/64; HP for conv SR2, 8/7/64; 543 Sqn, 23/3/65; HP, 20/12/67; HS, 10/6/70; Min Tech, 16/9/70; HS for conv K2, 3/9/71; 232 OCU, 12/5/75; 55 Sqn, 3/7/75.

82. XM716. Aw C, 28/2/63; 139 Sqn, 5/3/63; 100 Sqn, 23/10/63; 232 OCU, 28/4/64; HP for conv SR2, 5/8/64; 543 Sqn, 2/11/65; flying accident — crashed at Warboys, 29/6/66; SOC, 30/6/66.

83. XM717. Aw C, 12/3/63; 100 Sqn, 14/3/63; HP for conv B2R, 20/3/64; Wittering Wg, 9/2/65; 543 Sqn, 7/1/69; HS for conv K2, 13/3/74; 55 Sqn, 1/11/77; 57 Sqn, 12/2/85; 55 Sqn, 14/4/86.

84. XM718. Aw C, 30/4/63; 100 Sqn, 2/5/63; flying accident — brake chute deployed on approach, heavy landing at Wittering, 21/10/63; HP for repair, 5/12/63; partial conversion to SR2 (still retained Blue Steel control panel); MoA, 2/4/65; 543 Sqn, 3/1/66; 232 OCU, 24/9/74; Marham, 23/10/75; SOC, 31/3/76.

Cancelled Victor B2 Serials
XM719-XM721; XM745-XM756; XM785-XM794.
There were reported sightings of 'XL250-XL255' on the Radlett production line in March 1962, but these cannot be substantiated because these were never official serial allocations.

The Gulf War of 1990

In August 1990, No 55 Squadron was supporting RAF Jaguars at a reconnaissance Air Meet in Texas when all Victors were recalled to the UK in response to the Iraqi invasion of Kuwait. Within 24 hours they were back at Marham, and 48 hours later they were operating over France and Sicily deploying the fast jets to the Gulf.

At 22.50hrs GMT on 16 January 1991, two Victors led the first Murarraq-based Tornado GR1s, loaded with airfield-denial weapons, on bombing missions into Iraq. They operated along the Olive Trail, which ran generally south of the Iraq border before turning on to a short northerly leg and casting off the receiving bombers into the heart of Iraq territory.

On 19 January, an additional Victor was deployed to the Gulf. The Victor trio was to fly 138 Olive Trails in all, plus many other missions over the Persian Gulf to support attack aircraft and air defence patrols. Victors dispensed over 8,000,000lb of fuel in 290 sorties during the 42-day war.

Victor Data

Dimensions (ft/in)	HP80	B1/1A	B2
Overall length			
(nose to tail bullet)	98ft 2in	102ft 11in (B1A/K1A — 102ft 5in)	
(nose to tip of swept tail)		114ft 11in	114ft 11in
Wing span	110ft	110ft	120ft (K2 — 117ft)
Wing area	2,406sq ft	2,406sq ft	2,600sq ft
Height	28ft	26ft 9in	26ft 9in
Wheel track			
(centre of oleos)	30ft 2in	30ft 2in	33ft 2in
Tail Span	32ft 8in	32ft 8in	32ft 8in
Engines	4 × Sapphire Sa6	4 × Sapphire Sa7-20201 or 20701	4 × Conway Co11-10101/Co17-20101
Max speed	255kt/0.9M	330kt/0.93M	325kt/0.92M
Weight limitations (lb)			
Max take-off	104,000	185,000	204,000 (223,000 with drop tanks) (K2 — 238,000 when operationally essential)
Max emergency landing	104,000	185,000	200,000 (K2 — 238,000)
Max normal landing	86,500	135,000	145,000 (K2 — 150,000)

Selected Bibliography

Barnes, C. H., *Handley Page Aircraft Since 1907*, Putnam, 1976.
British Aviation Research Group, *Falklands — The Air War*, 1986.
Brookes, Andrew, *V-Force*, Jane's, 1982.
Ethell, J. and Price, A., *Air War South Atlantic*, Sedgwick and Jackson, 1983.
Gunston, Bill, *Bombers of the West*, Ian Allan, 1973.
Gunston, Bill, *The V Bombers*, *Aerospace Monthly*, January-March 1981.
Lee, Godfrey, *Unassailable Aerodynamical Logic*, *Aerospace*, October and November 1976.
Middlebrook, Martin, *Operation Corporate*, Viking, 1985.
ap Rees, Elfan, *Handley Page Victor*, *Air Pictorial*, May and June 1972.

I would also like to pay tribute to everyone who has given of their time to help in compiling this book, with particular thanks to Harry Fraser-Mitchell, Steve Millard, Paul Jackson and Roger Brooks for their unstinting assistance, and to James Goulding for his drawings.